Little Passenger®

Activity Books • Activity Maps

These games and puzzles were designed to make time fly while traveling.

Table of Contents

Alabama	3	Nebraska	29
Alaska	4	Nevada	30
Arizona	5	New Hampshire	31
Arkansas	6	New Jersey	34
California	7	New Mexico	35
Canada	55	New York	36
Colorado	8	North Carolina	37
Connecticut	9	North Dakota	38
Delaware	10	Ohio	39
Florida	11	Oklahoma	40
Georgia	12	Oregon	41
Hawaii	13	Pennsylvania	42
Idaho	14	Rhode Island	43
Illinois	15	South Carolina	44
Indiana	16	South Dakota	45
Iowa	17	Tennessee	46
Kansas	18	Texas	47
Kentucky	19	Utah	48
Louisiana	20	Vermont	49
Maine	21	Virginia	50
Maryland	22	Washington	51
Massachusetts	23	West Virginia	52
Mexico	56	Wisconsin	53
Michigan	24	Wyoming	54
Minnesota	25	U.S.A. Map	32-33
Mississippi	26	Answer Pages	63-64
Missouri	27	Index	57-62
Montana	28		

ALABAMA

Heart of Dixie, Camellia State

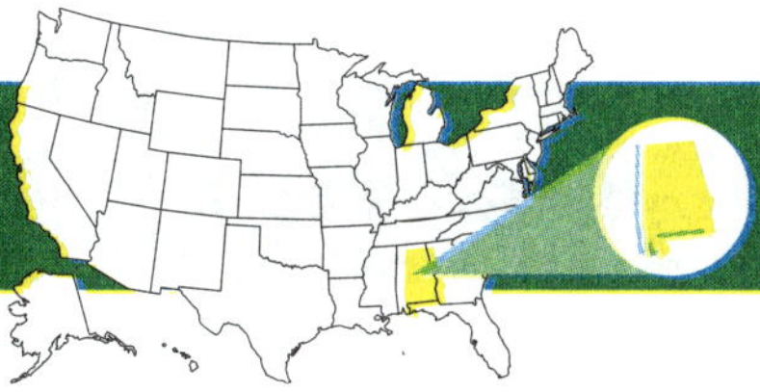

CROSSWORD

Alabama's capital is Montgomery. Use the cities on the map to complete the puzzle.

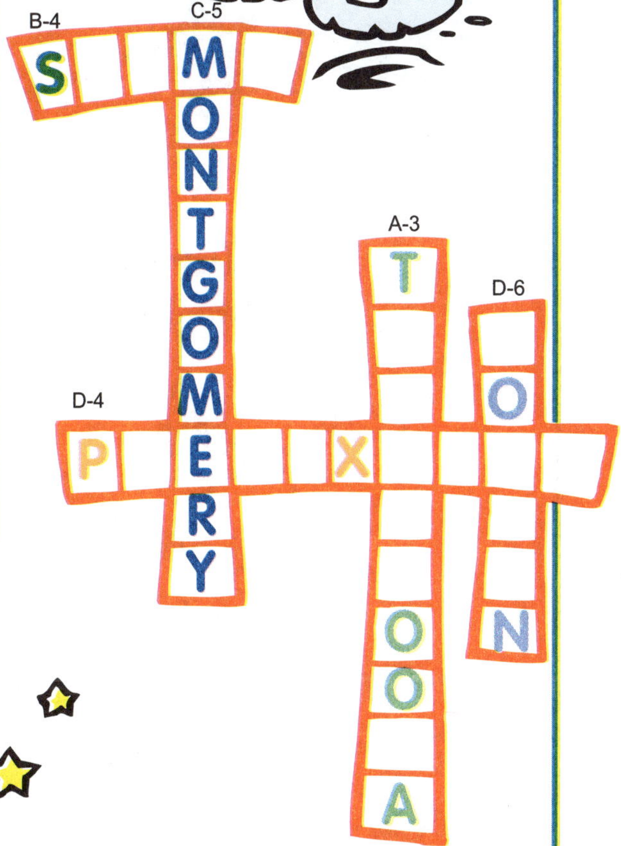

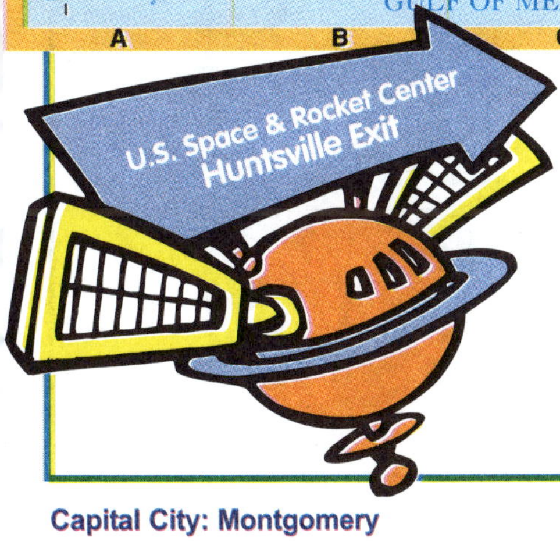

Capital City: Montgomery
State Bird: Yellowhammer
State Tree: Southern Pine
Statehood: 1819
State Flower: Camellia

ALASKA
The Last Frontier

Map of Alaska with grid coordinates A–F and 1–5, showing cities, regions, and geographic features.

MATCHING
Find the two that match.

Capital City: Juneau
State Bird: Willow Ptarmigan
State Tree: Sitka Spruce
Statehood: 1959
State Flower: Forget-Me-Not

ARIZONA
Grand Canyon State

COLOR-BY-NUMBER

1= Red
2= Green
3= Brown
4= Yellow
5= Blue
6= Gray

ARKANSAS

The Natural State, The Razorback State

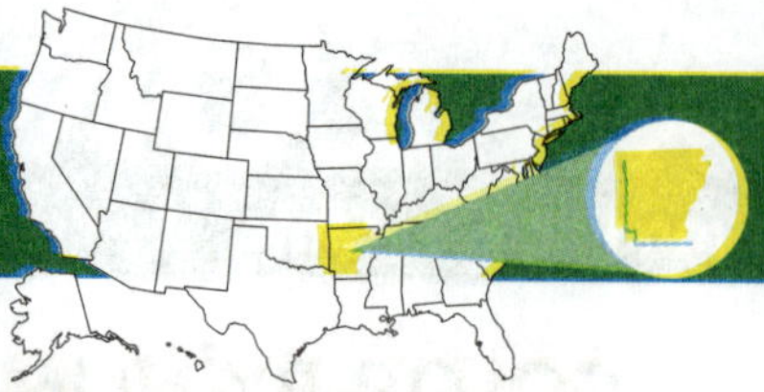

DECODER PUZZLE

Decode the puzzle to name this national park in Arkansas.

3 1 6   5 8 2 4 7 9 5

1=O 3=H 5=S 7=N 9=G

2=R 4=I 6=T 8=P

Capital City: Little Rock
State Bird: Mockingbird
State Tree: Pine
Statehood: 1836
State Flower: Apple Blossom

CALIFORNIA

Golden State

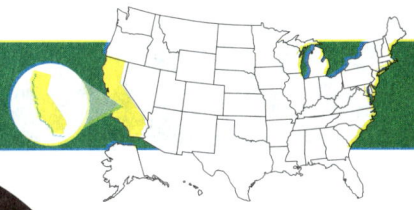

ART PROJECT

Design a T-shirt featuring all the fun things there are to do in California.

Capital City: Sacramento
State Bird: California Valley Quail

State Tree: California Redwood

Statehood: 1850
State Flower: Golden Poppy

COLORADO
Centennial State

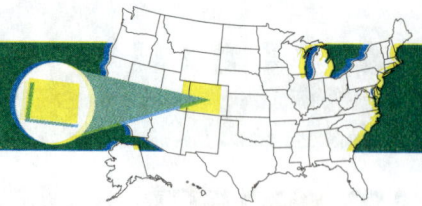

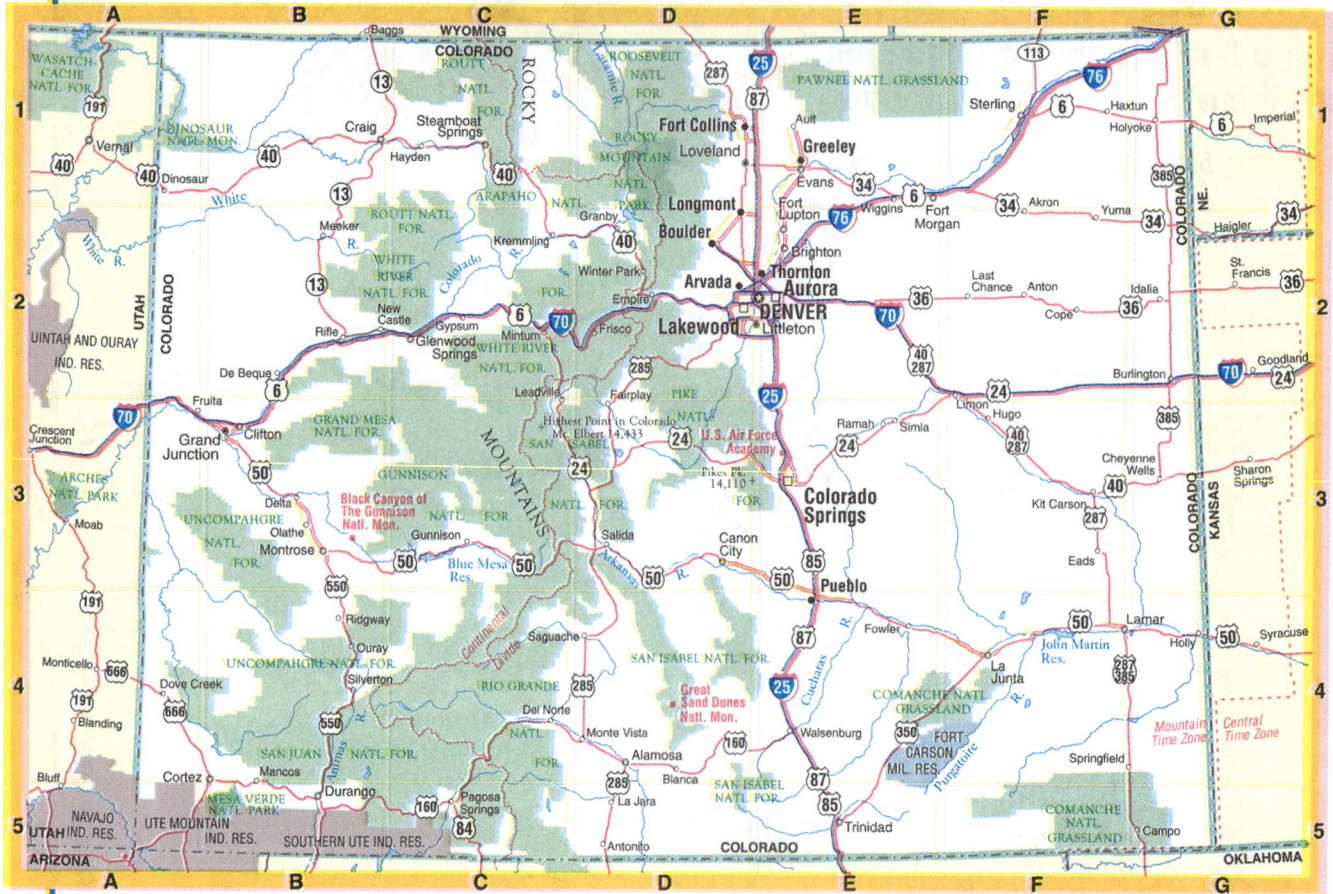

PUZZLE-IN-THE-ROUND
Start at W and write every other letter to name Colorado's neighboring states.

1. _____

2. _____

3. _____

4. _____

5. _____

6. _____

7. _____

Capital City: Denver

State Bird: Lark Bunting

State Tree: Colorado Blue Spruce

Statehood: 1876

State Flower: Rocky Mtn. Columbine

CONNECTICUT

Constitution State, Nutmeg State

WORD SMITH

How many words can you make from the letters in CONNECTICUT?

_____   _____
_____   _____
_____   _____
_____   _____
_____   _____

Capital City: Hartford

State Bird: American Robin   **State Tree: White Oak**

Statehood: 1788

State Flower: Mountain Laurel

DELAWARE
First State, Diamond State

COUNTING
Count the crabs.

Write your answer here.

Capital City: Dover

State Bird: Blue Hen Chicken

State Tree: American Holly

Statehood: 1787

State Flower: Peach Blossom

FLORIDA

Sunshine State

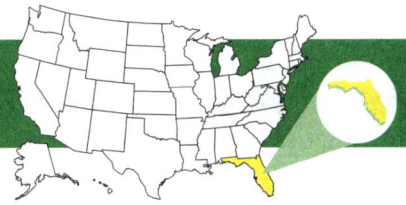

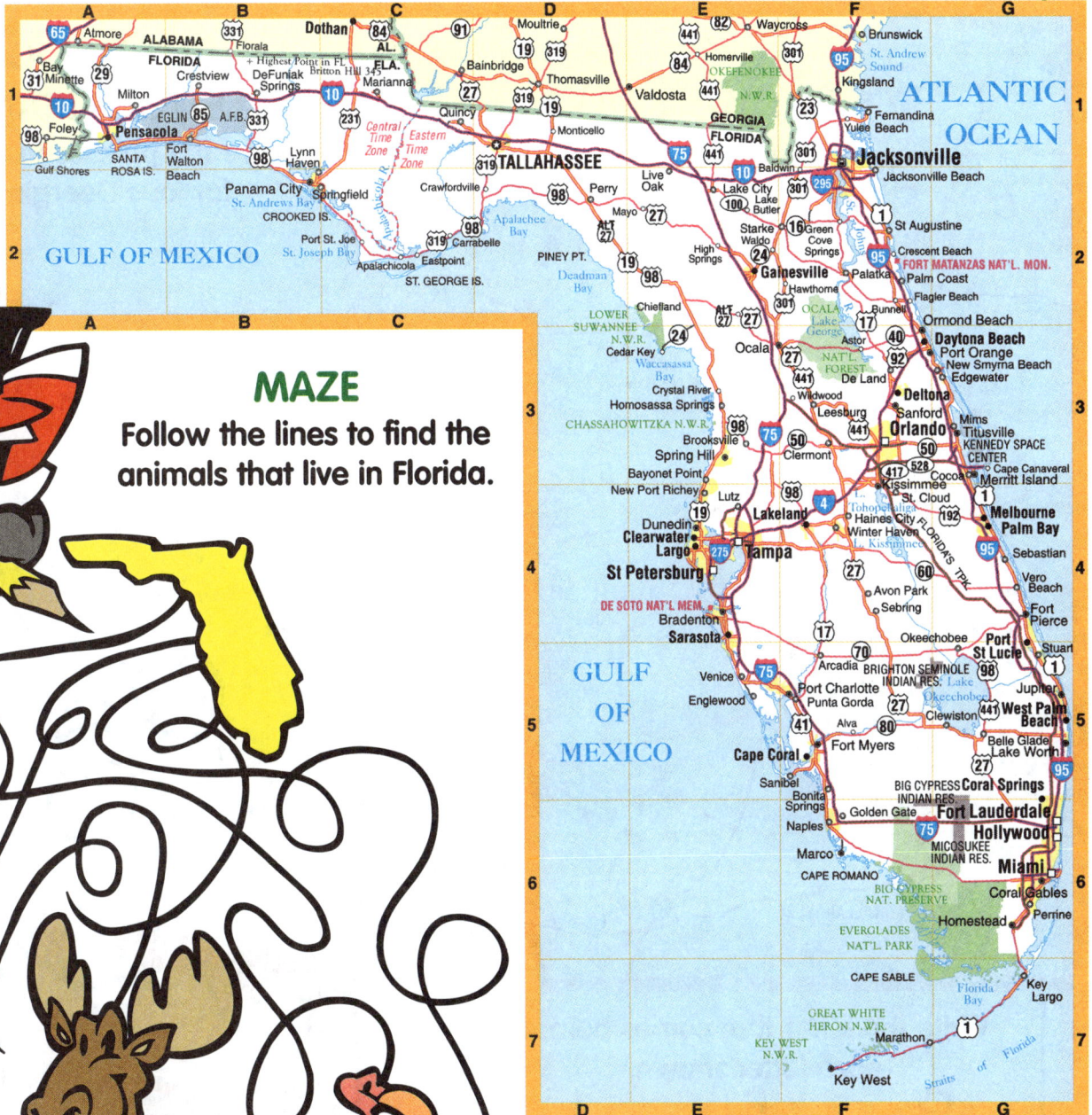

MAZE

Follow the lines to find the animals that live in Florida.

Capital City: Tallahassee
State Bird: Mockingbird
State Tree: Sabal Palmetto Palm
Statehood: 1845
State Flower: Orange Blossom

GEORGIA

Empire State of the South, Peach State

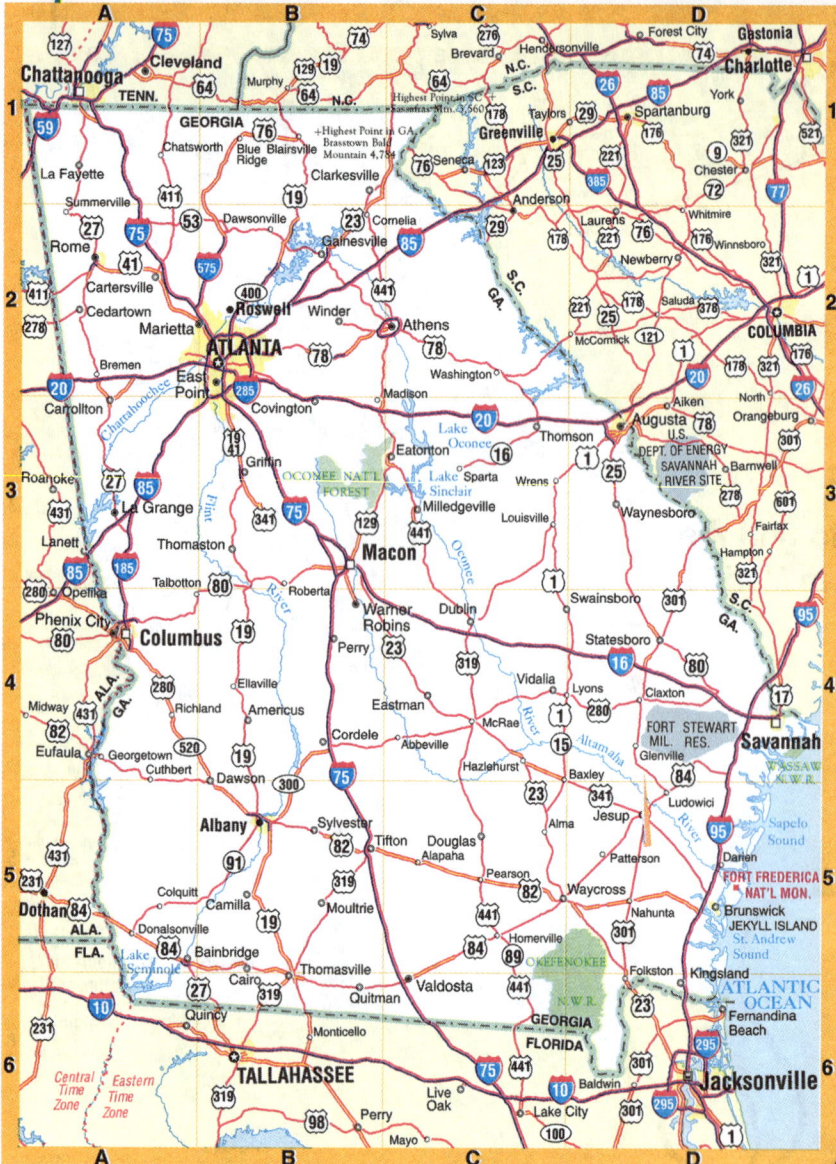

DOT-TO-DOT & LETTER SCRAMBLE

Solve the puzzles to name this famous Georgia fruit.

Write the letter that comes before each letter shown.

Q   F   B   D   I

Capital City: Atlanta
State Bird: Brown Thrasher
State Tree: Live Oak
Statehood: 1788
State Flower: Cherokee Rose

HAWAII
Aloha State

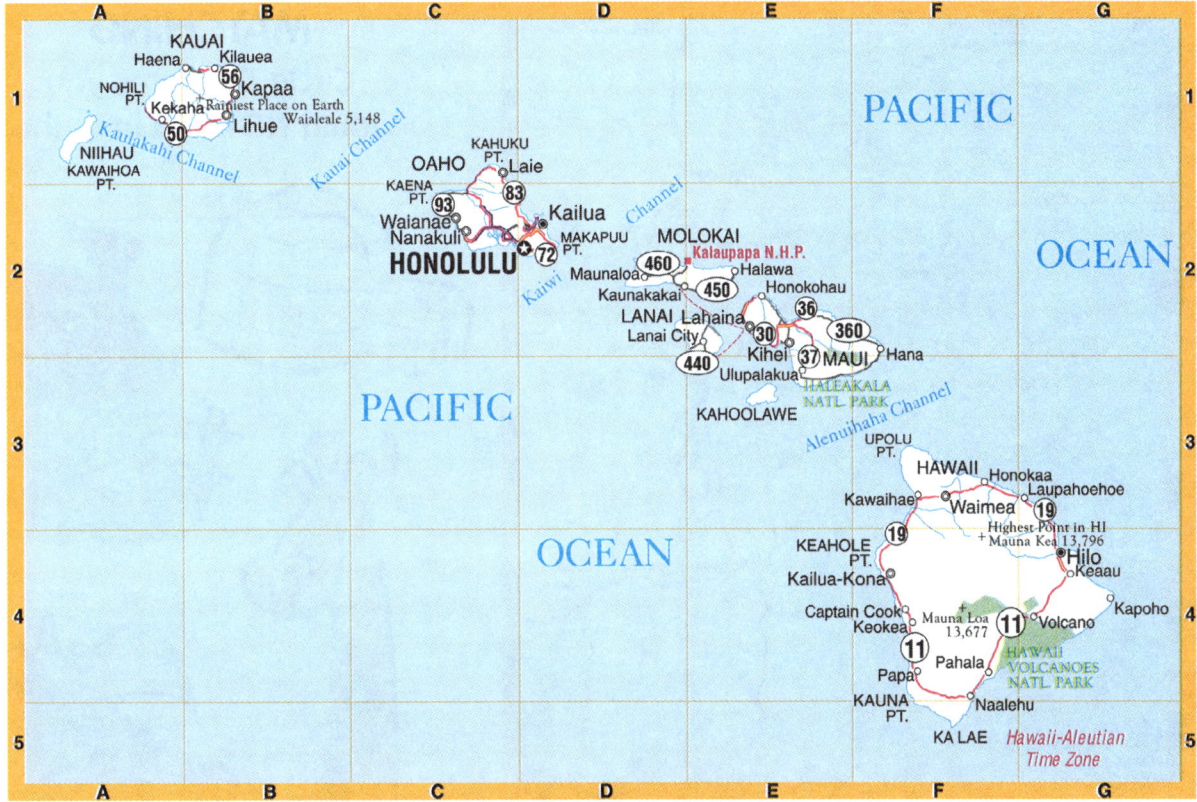

Map labels:

KAUAI — Haena, Kilauea, Kapaa, NOHILI PT., Kekaha, Lihue, 56, 50, Rainiest Place on Earth Waialeale 5,148, Kaulakahi Channel, NIIHAU, KAWAIHOA PT.

Kauai Channel

OAHO — KAHUKU PT., Laie, KAENA PT., 93, 83, Kailua, Waianae, Nanakuli, MAKAPUU PT., 72, **HONOLULU**, Kaiwi Channel

MOLOKAI — Kalaupapa N.H.P., 460, Halawa, Maunaloa, 450, Honokohau, Kaunakakai, 36, **LANAI** Lahaina, 30, 360, Lanai City, Kihei, 37, **MAUI**, Hana, 440, Ulupalakua, HALEAKALA NATL PARK, **KAHOOLAWE**, Alenuihaha Channel

PACIFIC OCEAN

UPOLU PT., **HAWAII**, Honokaa, Laupahoehoe, Kawaihae, Waimea, 19, Highest Point in HI + Mauna Kea 13,796, KEAHOLE PT., 19, Hilo, Keaau, Kailua-Kona, Captain Cook, Mauna Loa 13,677, Keokea, 11, Volcano, Kapoho, 11, Pahala, HAWAII VOLCANOES NATL PARK, Papa, KAUNA PT., Naalehu, KA LAE, Hawaii-Aleutian Time Zone

PACIFIC OCEAN

MEMORY GAME

Look at the page for 30 seconds.
Turn to page 63 to list all the things you remember.

13

Capital City: Honolulu

State Bird: Hawaiian Goose

State Tree: Kukui (Candlenut)

Statehood: 1959

State Flower: Yellow Hibiscus

IDAHO
Gem State

14

Capital City: Boise
State Bird: Mountain Bluebird

State Tree: White Pine

Statehood: 1890
State Flower: Syringa

ILLINOIS
Prairie State

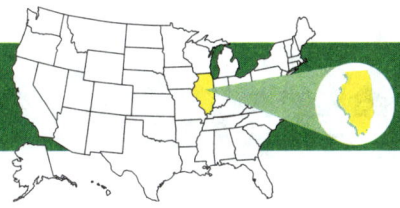

MAPPING SKILLS

Use the index on page 58 to fill in the grid coordinates for these cities.

GRID COORDINATE

Champaign _____

Chicago _____

Decatur _____

Paris _____

Rock Falls _____

Springfield _____

Waterloo _____

15

Capital City: Springfield
State Bird: Cardinal
State Tree: White Oak
Statehood: 1818
State Flower: Native Violet

INDIANA

Hoosier State

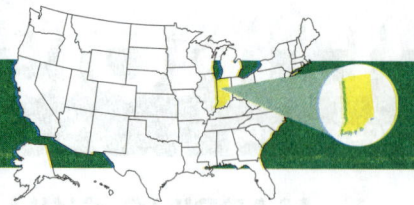

COLORING

Indianapolis is the home of the Indy 500. Color Sparky's race car with your favorite colors.

Map cities and features

Chicago, Joliet, Gary, Michigan City, South Bend, Mishawaka, Niles, Sturgis, MICH., IND., OHIO, Elkhart, Lagrange, Angola, La Porte, Valparaiso, Walkerton, Goshen, Kendallville, Auburn, Plymouth, Knox, Warsaw, Churubusco, Columbia City, Fort Wayne, Medaryville, Winamac, Rensselaer, Kentland, Logansport, Huntington, Decatur, Monticello, Peru, Wabash, Delphi, Marion, Portland, Lafayette, Kokomo, Frankfort, Alexandria, Muncie, Winchester, Lynn, Attica, Veedersburg, Anderson, Noblesville, New Castle, Highest Point in IN, Crawfordsville, Lebanon, Brownsburg, INDIANAPOLIS, Greenfield, Knightstown, Richmond, Rockville, Liberty, Greencastle, Mooresville, Terre Haute, Franklin, Rushville, Spencer, Nashville, Greensburg, Worthington, Sullivan, Bloomington, Columbus, Versailles, Aurora, Seymour, North Vernon, Bedford, Brownstown, Madison, Bicknell, Loogootee, Washington, Paoli, Jasper, Palmyra, New Albany, Jeffersonville, FRANKFORT, Louisville, Princeton, Huntingburg, Dale, Evansville, Mount Vernon, Henderson, Owensboro, Morganfield, Kankakee, Watseka, Rantoul, Danville, Chrisman, Paris, Lawrenceville, Olney, Mount Carmel, Irvington, Bardstown, Harrodsburg, Elizabethtown

Central Time Zone, Eastern Time Zone

ILLINOIS, INDIANA, KENTUCKY

Monroe L., HOOSIER NAT'L FOR., HOOSIER NAT'L FOREST, LINCOLN BOYHOOD NAT'L MEM., Rough River Lake, Patoka R., Wabash River, White R., Blue R.

16

Capital City: Indianapolis
State Bird: Cardinal
State Tree: Tulip Poplar
Statehood: 1816
State Flower: Peony

IOWA

Hawkeye State

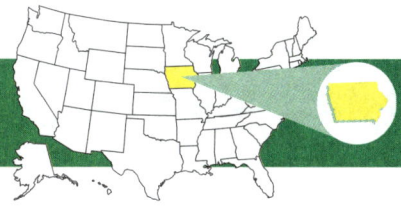

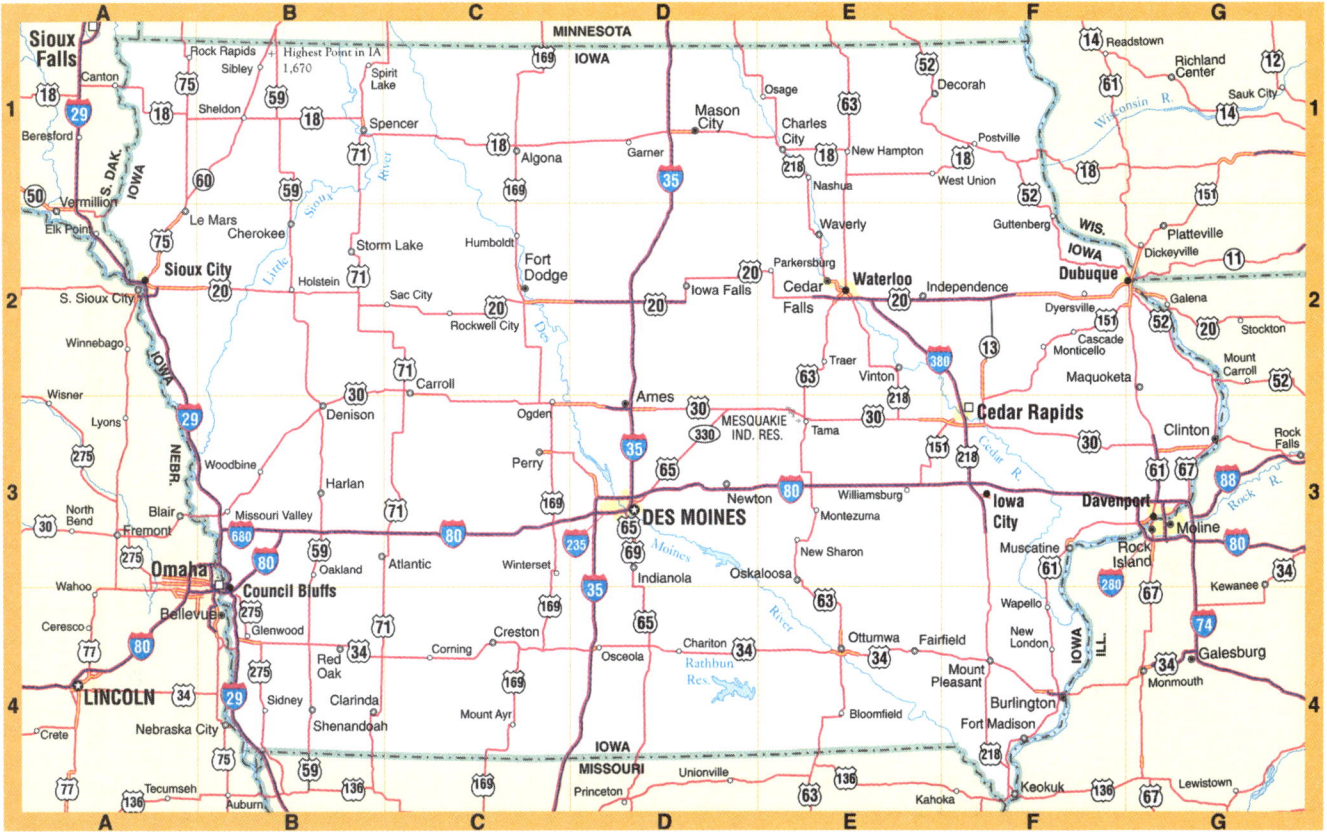

Map of Iowa showing cities and highways, bordered by Minnesota, South Dakota, Nebraska, Missouri, Wisconsin, and Illinois.

Cities and labels visible on the map include: Sioux Falls, Canton, Rock Rapids, Sibley, Highest Point in IA 1,670, Spirit Lake, Readstown, Richland Center, Sauk City, Beresford, Sheldon, Spencer, Algona, Garner, Mason City, Osage, Charles City, New Hampton, Postville, Decorah, Vermillion, Le Mars, Cherokee, Storm Lake, Humboldt, Fort Dodge, Iowa Falls, Nashua, Waverly, West Union, Guttenberg, Platteville, Dickeyville, Elk Point, Sioux City, Holstein, Sac City, Cedar Falls, Parkersburg, Waterloo, Independence, Dubuque, Galena, S. Sioux City, Rockwell City, Dyersville, Cascade, Monticello, Maquoketa, Mount Carroll, Stockton, Winnebago, Carroll, Ames, Traer, Vinton, Cedar Rapids, Clinton, Rock Falls, Wisner, Denison, Ogden, Mesquakie Ind. Res., Tama, Lyons, Harlan, Perry, Newton, Williamsburg, Iowa City, Davenport, Moline, North Bend, Blair, Missouri Valley, Des Moines, Montezuma, Rock Island, Fremont, Woodbine, Oakland, Atlantic, Winterset, Indianola, New Sharon, Muscatine, Kewanee, Omaha, Bellevue, Council Bluffs, Glenwood, Creston, Oskaloosa, Wapello, New London, Galesburg, Wahoo, Ceresco, Red Oak, Corning, Osceola, Chariton, Ottumwa, Fairfield, Mount Pleasant, Monmouth, Lincoln, Sidney, Clarinda, Shenandoah, Mount Ayr, Bloomfield, Burlington, Fort Madison, Crete, Nebraska City, Tecumseh, Auburn, Unionville, Princeton, Keokuk, Lewiston, Kahoka.

WHAT'S WRONG WITH THIS PICTURE?

Circle all the things wrong with this picture.

17

Capital City: **Des Moines**

State Bird: **Eastern Goldfinch**

State Tree: **Oak**

Statehood: **1846**

State Flower: **Wild Rose**

KANSAS

Sunflower State

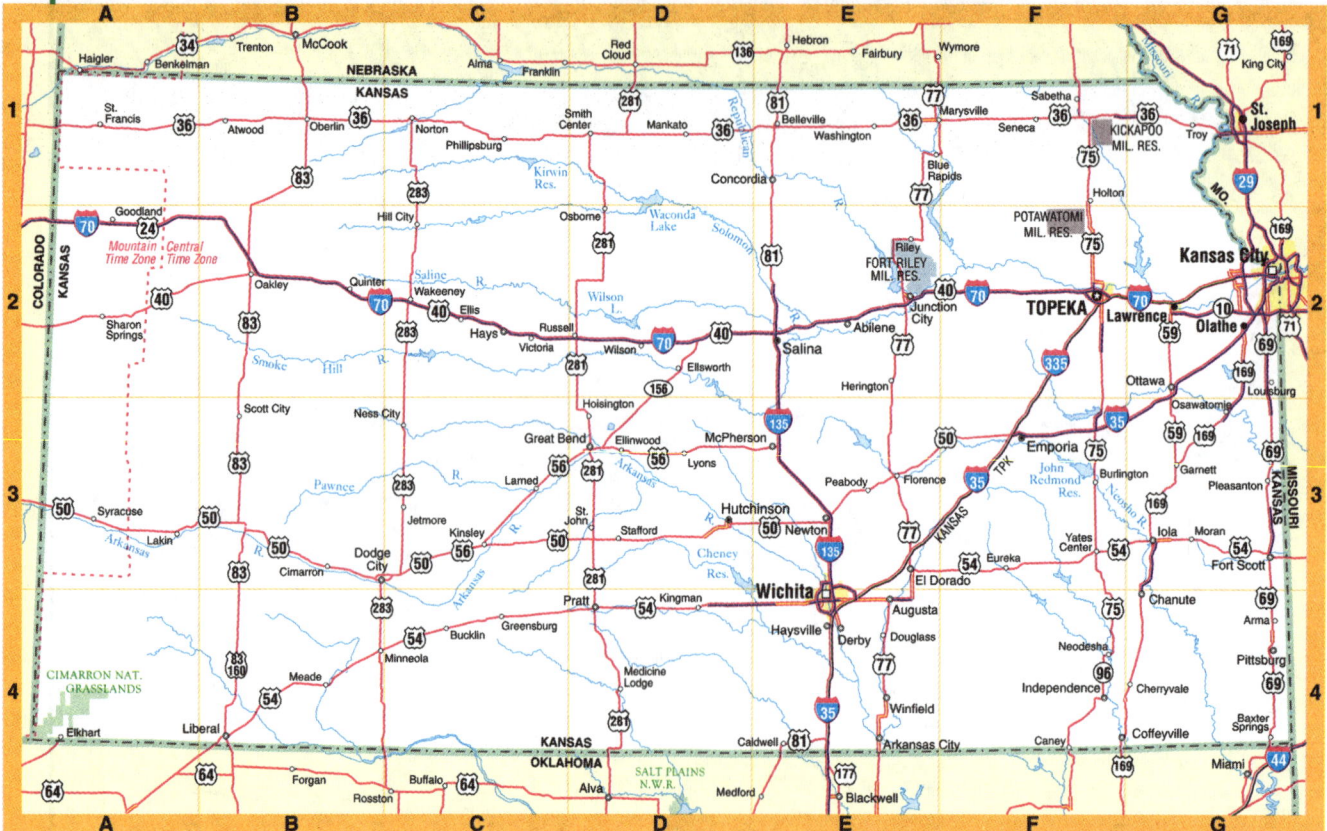

KANSAS

WORD SCRAMBLE

Cross out all of the X's, Z's and O's to spell the name of this famous lawman.

XZXWZXYOXOAOXXOTZOZTX

XZEOXAORZXXPOZ

– – – – – – – – – – –

– – – – – – – –

Capital City: Topeka

State Bird: Western Meadowlark

State Tree: Cottonwood

Statehood: 1861

State Flower: Native Sunflower

KENTUCKY
Bluegrass State

DECODER PUZZLE
Write the first letter of each item to name this famous Kentucky frontiersman.

Capital City: Frankfort
State Bird: Cardinal
State Tree: Tulip Poplar
Statehood: 1792
State Flower: Goldenrod

LOUISIANA
Pelican State

WORD SEARCH

Jean Lafitte was a famous pirate. How many times does the word "PIRATE" appear?

P	G	D	F	E	K	P	I	R	A	T	E
I	E	B	X	R	Y	Y	G	F	M	P	F
R	G	F	J	D	E	T	A	R	I	P	F
A	H	C	R	G	C	N	U	R	F	Y	D
T	P	F	F	T	A	B	E	R	V	J	H
E	H	P	I	R	A	T	E	D	D	I	Y
H	T	H	F	D	A	F	K	C	E	L	E
U	M	J	D	R	T	D	O	G	S	O	T
K	L	T	I	P	I	R	A	T	E	U	A
A	Y	P	E	T	N	Z	L	J	S	J	R
Q	E	G	S	G	G	A	Y	K	Q	G	I
E	T	A	R	I	P	A	R	I	P	H	P

Remember, the word can appear forwards, backwards, up, down, and diagonally.

20

Capital City: Baton Rouge
State Bird: Eastern Brown Pelican
State Tree: Cypress
Statehood: 1812
State Flower: Magnolia

MAINE
Pine Tree State

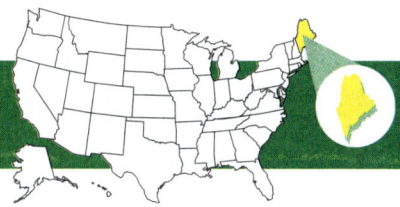

Map of Maine showing cities, roads, and geographic features with grid coordinates A–E and 1–7.

Key locations include: QUÉBEC, CANADA, Edmundston, Van Buren, St. Leonard, Grand Falls (Grand-Sault), Caribou, Presque Isle, Perth-Andover, Mars Hill, Monticello, Houlton, Woodstock, Nackawic, NEW BRUNSWICK, Danforth, Springfield, Topsfield, Lincoln, Woodland, Wesley, Perry, Whiting, Machias, Jonesboro, Cherryfield, Bangor, Amherst, Ellsworth, Bar Harbor, ACADIA NAT'L PARK, Pleasant Bay, Bucksport, Belfast, Camden, Stonington, Isle au Haut, Rockland, Thomaston, Wiscasset, AUGUSTA, Lewiston, Auburn, Brunswick, Bath, Gray, Yarmouth, Portland, Kittery, ATLANTIC OCEAN, MATINICUS ISLAND, Ferry To Yarmouth, Nova Scotia.

Western areas: Baie-Saint-Paul, Basilica of Ste. Anne De Beaupre, La Pocatière, Beaupré, Montmagny, Saint-Pamphile, Sainte-Marie, Lac-Etchemin, Beauceville, Saint-Georges, ALLAGASH WILDERNESS WATERWAY, Churchill Lake, Chamberlain Lake, Chesuncook Lake, Moosehead Lake, BAXTER STATE PARK, Grand Lake Matagamon, Pemadumcook Lake, Highest Point in ME + Mt. Katahdin 5,267, Jackman, Snow Mtn. 3,948, Flagstaff Lake, West Forks, Milo, Guilford, Lagrange, Bingham, Harmony, Skowhegan, Farmington, Waterville, Rumford, Newry, Bethel, Norway, Winthrop, Fryeburg, Sebago Lake, Hollis Center, Sanford, Alfred, NH, Nicatous Lake, W. Grand Lake.

MAZE
Help Sparky get through the maze.

21

Capital City: Augusta

State Bird: Chickadee

State Tree: Eastern White Pine

Statehood: 1820

State Flower: White Pine Cone & Tassel

MARYLAND

Old Line State, Free State

MATCHING
Circle the matching Orioles.

Capital City: Annapolis

State Bird: Baltimore Oriole

State Tree: White Oak

Statehood: 1788

State Flower: Black-eyed Susan

MASSACHUSETTS

Bay State, Old Colony

WORD SMITH

How many words can you make from the letters in MASSACHUSETTS?

_____   _____
_____   _____
_____   _____
_____   _____
_____   _____
_____   _____
_____   _____
_____   _____
_____   _____

Capital City: Boston

State Bird: Chickadee

State Tree: American Elm

Statehood: 1788

State Flower: Mayflower

MICHIGAN

Great Lakes State, Wolverine State

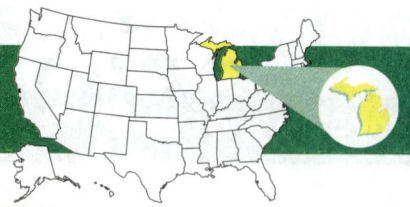

CROSSWORD

Use the map to complete the crossword of these Michigan lakes and solve the puzzle.

T _ _
  1 2

T
_ _ _ _
3 4 5 6

L _ K E _
7   8

Capital City: Lansing

State Bird: Robin

State Tree: White Pine

Statehood: 1837

State Flower: Apple Blossom

MINNESOTA

North Star State, Gopher State

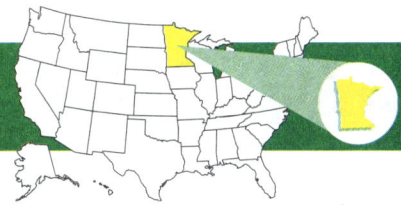

CITY SCRAMBLE

Unscramble the letters to name these Minnesota cities.

TS. OUDLC [B-4]

_ _ • _ _ _ _ _

DRE • GWIN [D-5]

_ _ _ • _ _ _ _

OANSCKJ [B-6]

_ _ _ _ _ _ _

OOKC [C-2]

_ _ _ _

UULDHT [D-3]

_ _ _ _ _ _

Capital City: St. Paul
State Bird: Common Loon

25

State Tree: Red Pine

Statehood: 1858
State Flower: Pink & White Lady's-slipper

MISSISSIPPI

Magnolia State

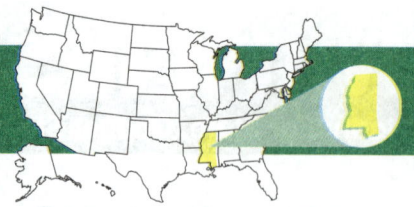

MATCHING

In honor of Mississippi, the Magnolia state, circle all the items that begin with the letter "M".

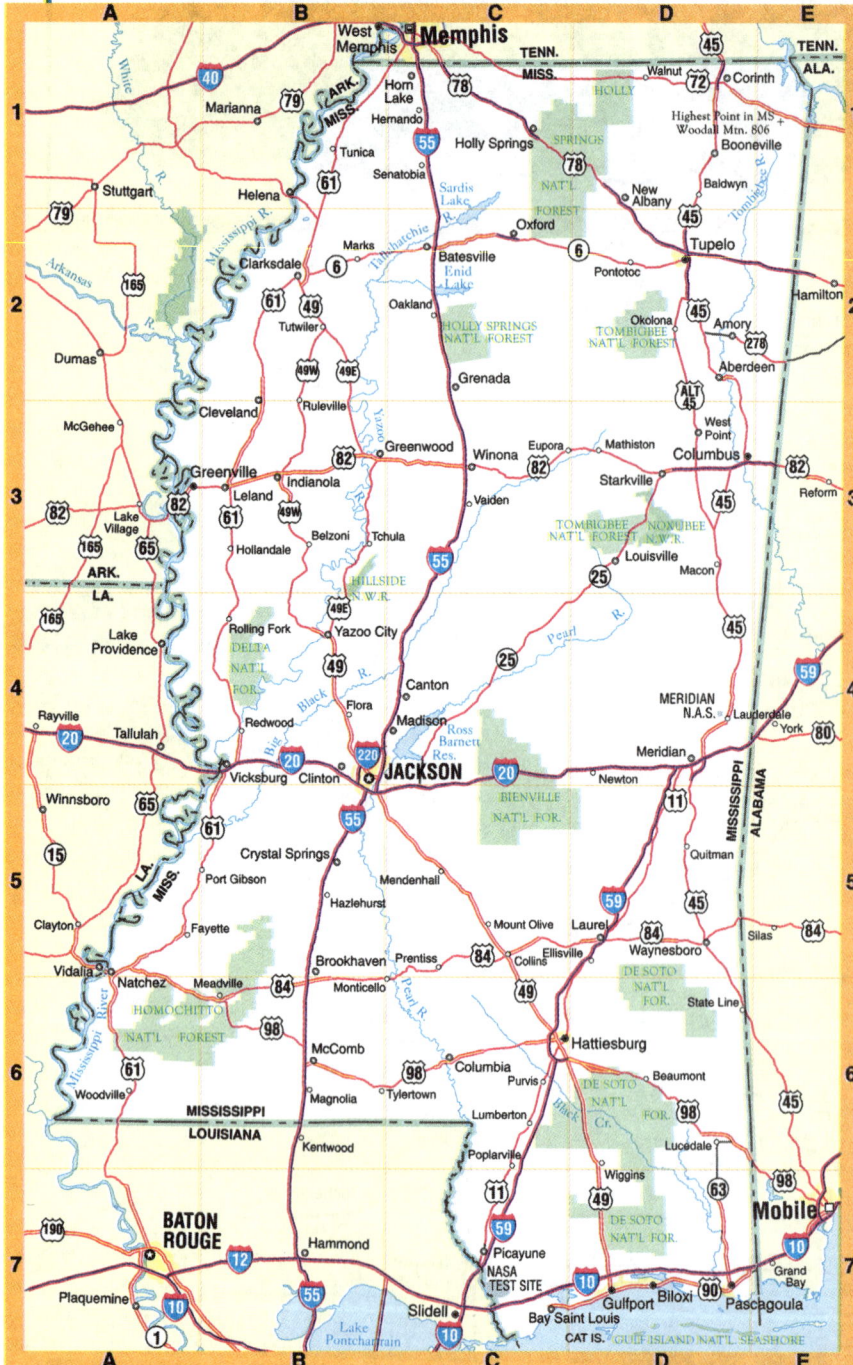

Capital City: Jackson
State Bird: Mockingbird
State Tree: Magnolia
Statehood: 1817
State Flower: Magnolia

MISSOURI

Show Me State

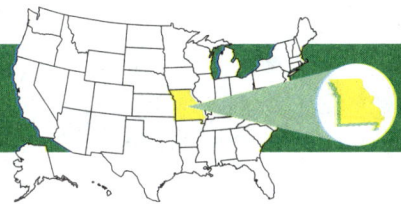

MAPPING

Use the map to complete the sentences.

1. Springfield is _____ of Joplin.
   East   South   West

2. Columbia is on U.S. _____.
   70   40   35

3. The capital city is marked with a _____.
   Star   triangle   X

4. St. Louis is near the _____ state border.
   Arkansas   Kansas   Illinois

27

Capital City: Jefferson City
State Bird: Bluebird
State Tree: Dogwood
Statehood: 1821
State Flower: Hawthorn

MONTANA
Treasure State

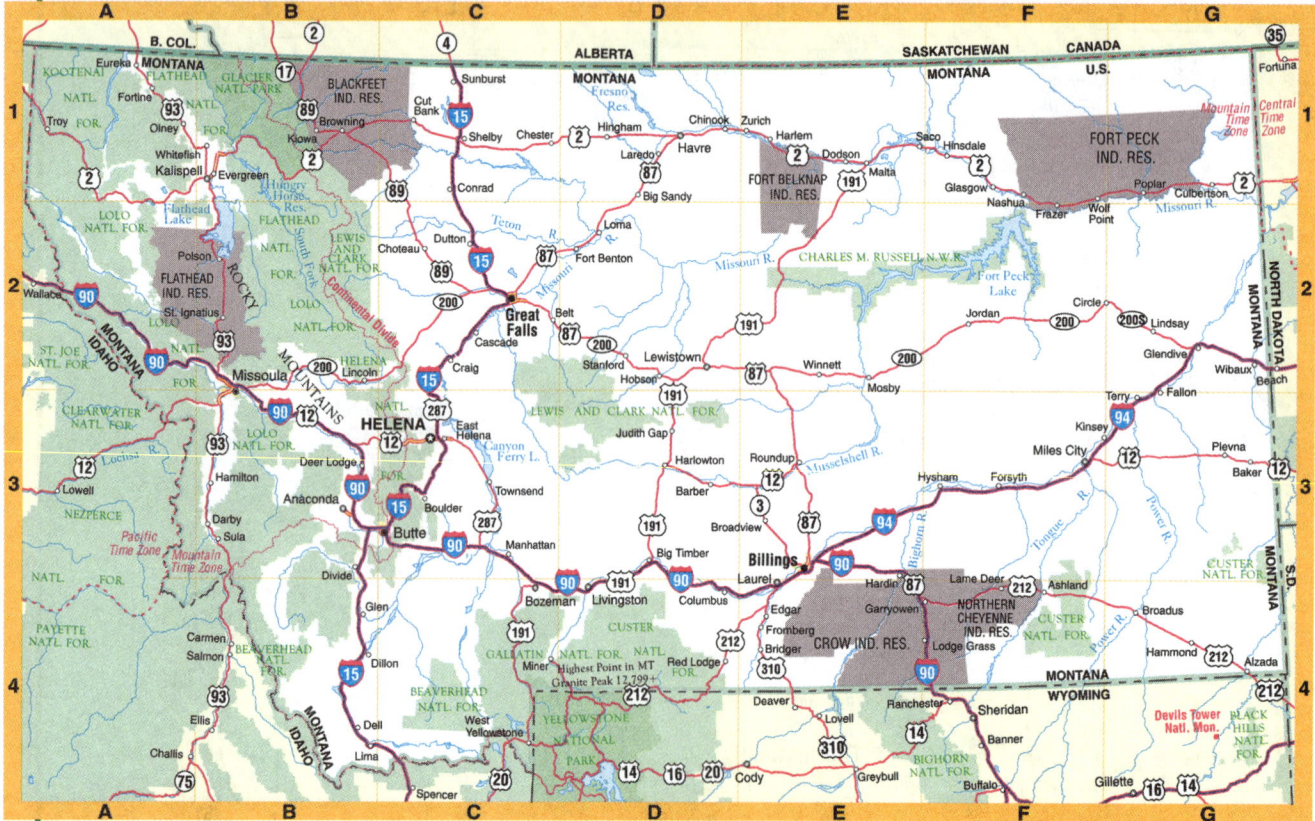

HIDDEN WORD

Color the blocks with an • dot yellow.
Color the blocks with a • dot black
to reveal the hidden word.

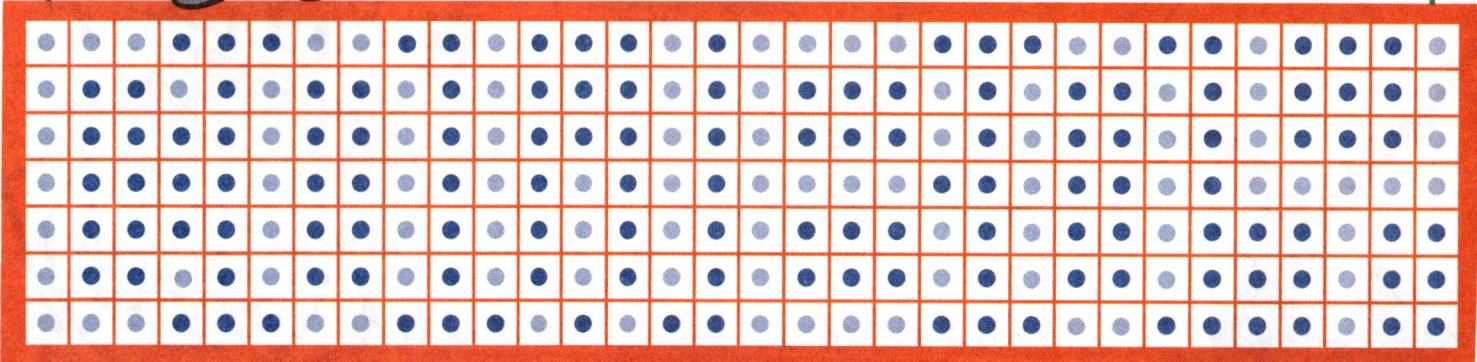

Capital City: Helena

State Bird: Western Meadowlark

State Tree: Ponderosa Pine

Statehood: 1889

State Flower: Bitterroot

NEBRASKA

Cornhusker State

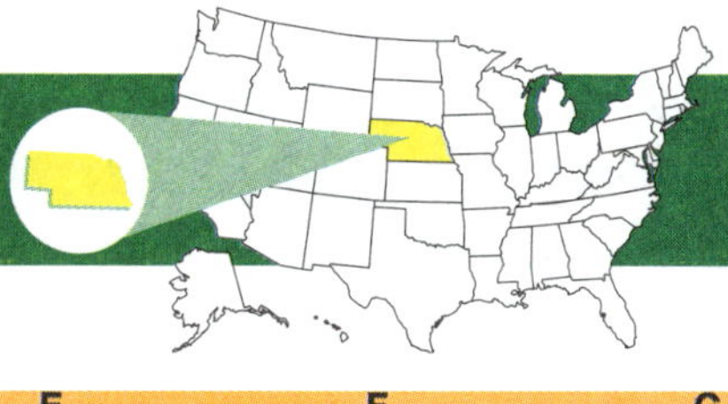

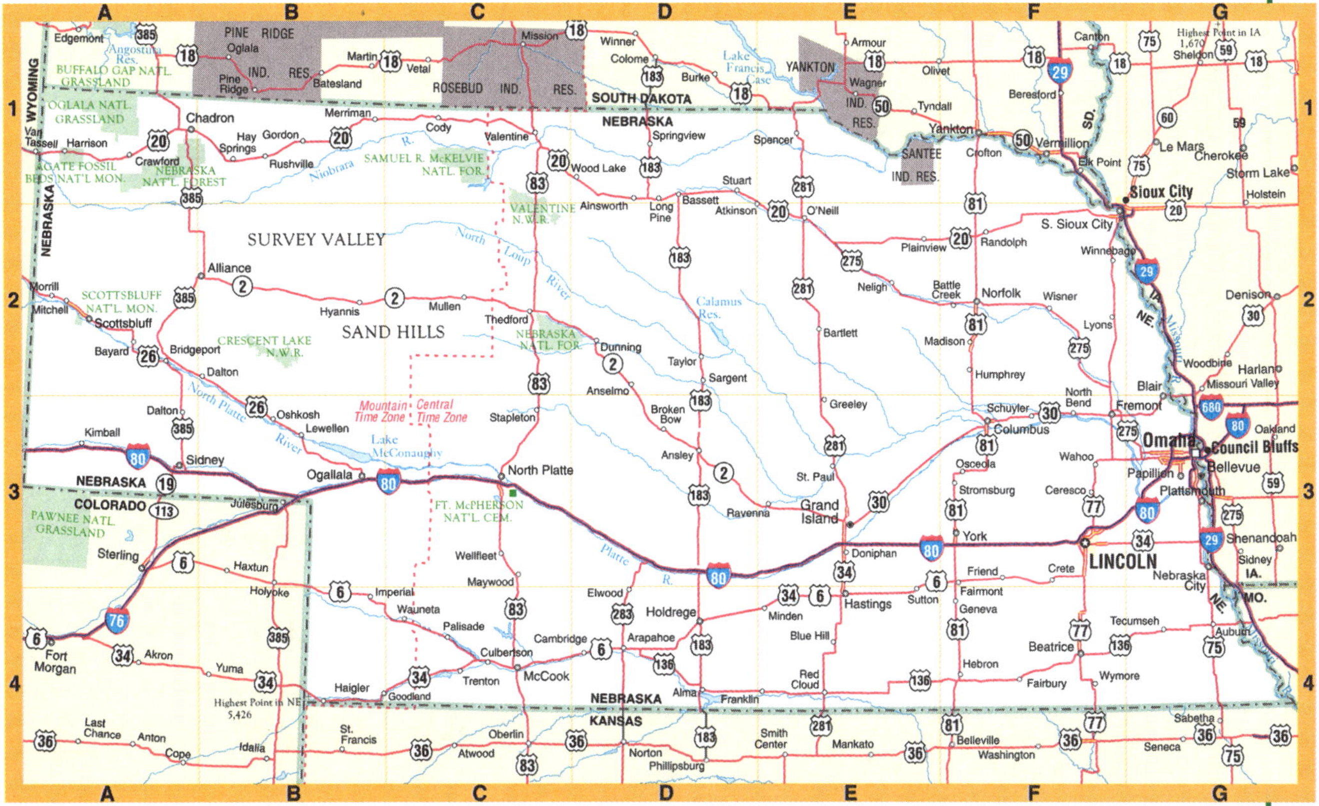

MAZE

Help Sparky find his way through the maze.

Capital City: Lincoln

State Bird: Western Meadowlark

State Tree: Cottonwood

Statehood: 1867

State Flower: Goldenrod

NEVADA

Sagebrush State, Battle Born State, Silver State

MAPPING SKILLS

Use the index on page 60 to fill in the grid coordinates for these cities.

	GRID COORDINATE
Austin	_____
Carson City	_____
Eureka	_____
Jackpot	_____
Reno	_____
Sparks	_____
Topaz Lake	_____

Capital City: Carson City
State Bird: Mountain Bluebird
State Trees: Single-leaf Piñon & Bristlecone Pine
Statehood: 1864
State Flower: Sagebrush

NEW HAMPSHIRE

Granite State

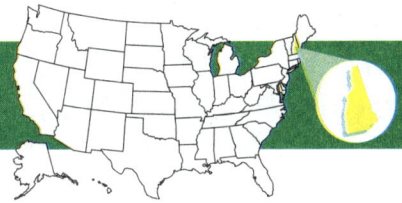

	State	Animal
Lancaster		
Concord		
Portsmouth		
Manchester		
Nashua		

ALPHABET SOUP

Using the first letter of the city, fill in the boxes. No word or name can be used more than once.

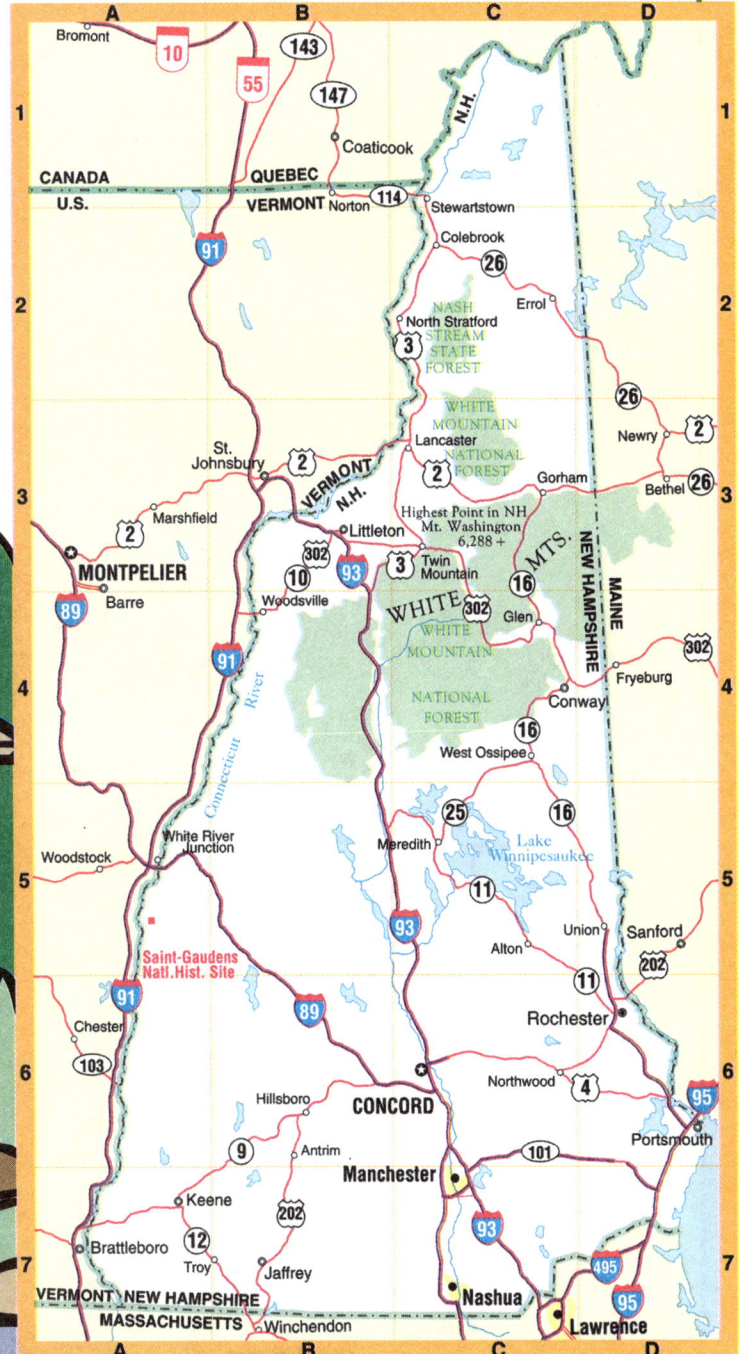

Capital City: Concord

State Bird: Purple Finch

State Tree: White Birch

Statehood: 1788

State Flower: Purple Lilac

U.S.A.

COLORING

Use your favorite colors to color the sights you might see as you travel across the U.S.A.

WASHINGTON
MONTANA
OREGON
CALIFORNIA
NEVADA
IDAHO
WYOMING
UTAH
ARIZONA
COLORADO
NEW MEXICO
NORTH DAKOTA
SOUTH DAKOTA
NEBRASKA
KANSAS
OKLAHOMA
TEXAS

Olympia
Seattle
Spokane
Portland
Salem
Boise
Reno
Sacramento
Oakland
San Francisco
San Diego
Los Angeles
Las Vegas
Phoenix
Tucson
Nogales
El Paso
Missoula
Great Falls
Helena
Butte
Billings
Idaho Falls
Pocatello
Casper
Salt Lake City
Cheyenne
Denver
Colorado Springs
Pueblo
Santa Fe
Albuquerque
Amarillo
Lubbock
Rapid City
Bismark
San Antonio
Laredo
Abilene

MEXICO

32

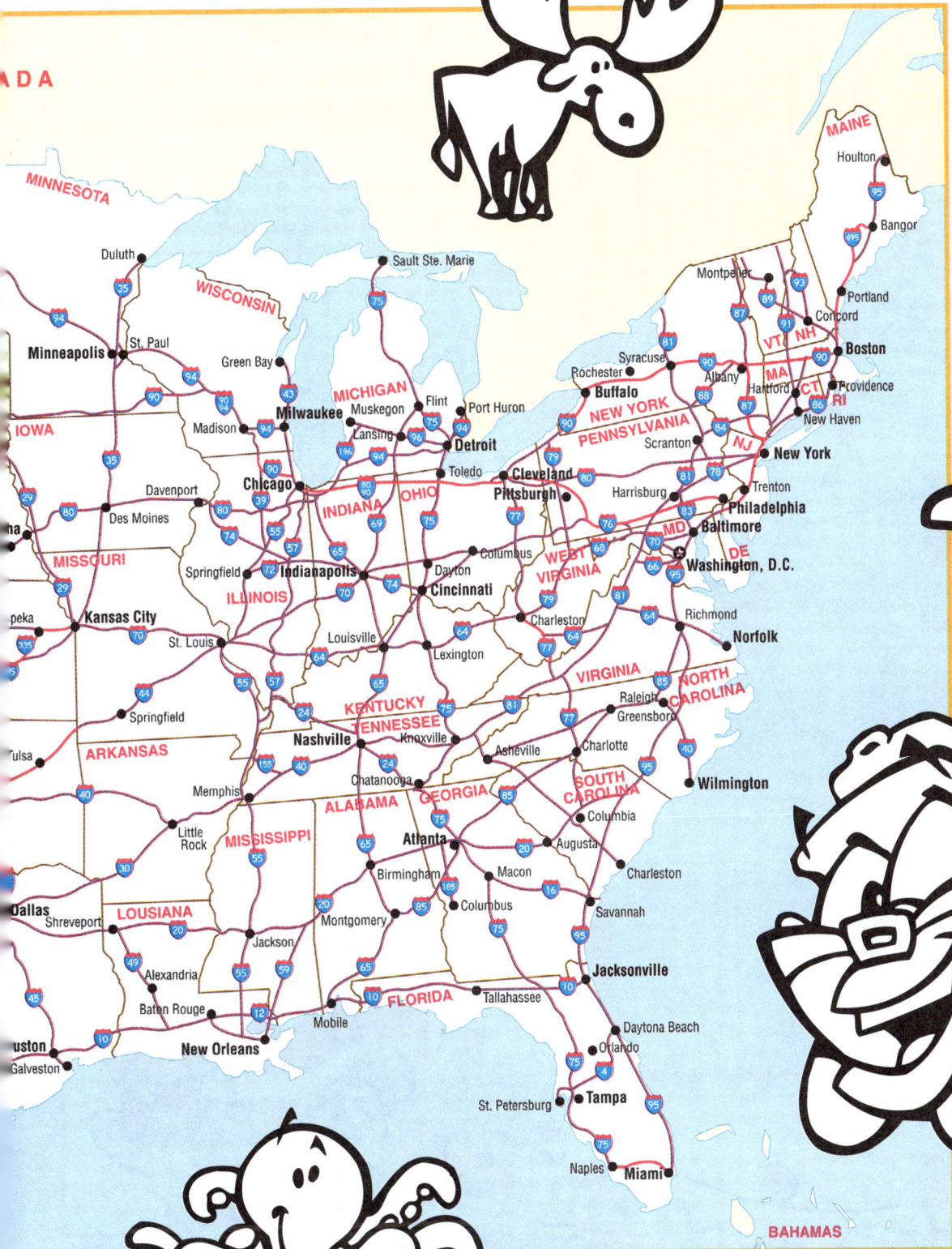

ADA

MINNESOTA

Duluth
Sault Ste. Marie

WISCONSIN

Minneapolis St. Paul
Green Bay

IOWA

Madison Milwaukee Muskegon Flint Port Huron

MICHIGAN

Lansing Detroit

Chicago Toledo Cleveland

INDIANA OHIO

Davenport

Des Moines

MISSOURI

Springfield Indianapolis Dayton Columbus

ILLINOIS Cincinnati

WEST VIRGINIA

Kansas City St. Louis Louisville Charleston

Lexington

peka

Springfield KENTUCKY VIRGINIA

Tulsa TENNESSEE Nashville Knoxville Raleigh

ARKANSAS NORTH CAROLINA

Asheville Charlotte Greensboro

Little Rock Chatanooga SOUTH CAROLINA Wilmington

Memphis GEORGIA Columbia

MISSISSIPPI ALABAMA Atlanta Augusta

Dallas Birmingham Macon Charleston

Shreveport LOUSIANA Montgomery Columbus Savannah

Alexandria Jackson

Baton Rouge Mobile FLORIDA Tallahassee Jacksonville

uston New Orleans Daytona Beach

Galveston Orlando

St. Petersburg Tampa

Naples Miami

MAINE

Houlton

Bangor

Montpelier Portland

Concord

VT NH Boston

Syracuse Albany MA Providence

Rochester Buffalo Hartford RI

NEW YORK New Haven

PENNSYLVANIA Scranton NJ New York

Pittsburgh Harrisburg Trenton

Philadelphia

MD Baltimore

DE

Washington, D.C.

Richmond

Norfolk

BAHAMAS

NEW JERSEY

Garden State

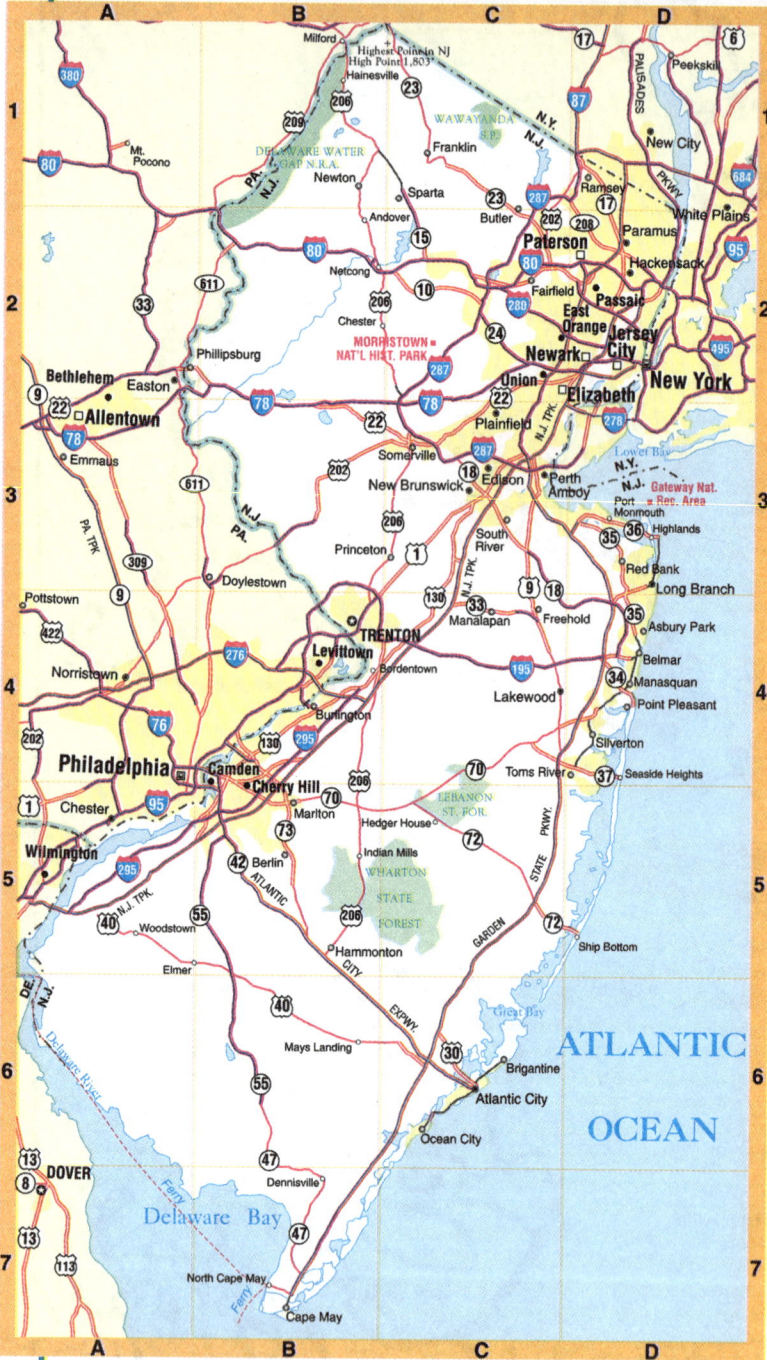

CROSSWORD

Use the cities on the map to complete the puzzle.

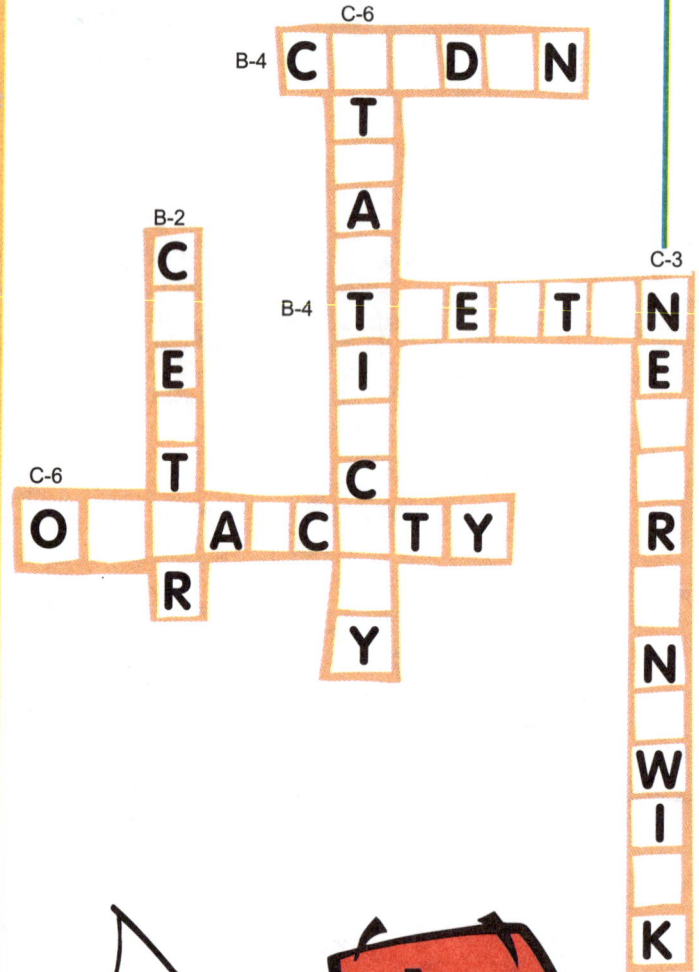

```
        C-6
B-4  C     D  N
     T
     A
 B-2  T          C-3
 C   B-4  T  E  T  N
 E        I        E
 T        C        R
 C-6      Y        R
 O  A  C  T  Y     N
 R                 W
 Y                 I
                   K
```

34

Capital City: Trenton
State Bird: Eastern Goldfinch
State Tree: Red Oak
Statehood: 1787
State Flower: Purple Violet

NEW MEXICO
Land of Enchantment

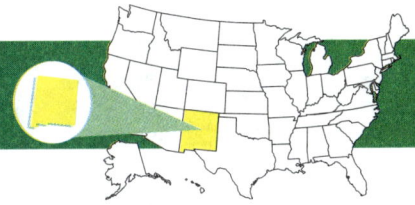

WORD SEARCH
Find and circle these New Mexico cities.

Word Bank
Albuquerque • Aztec • Farmington

Hobbs • Roswell • Santa Fe

```
A  O  S  N  N  P  F  T  E
E  H  W  E  I  T  A  S  G
E  A  E  F  N  I  R  E  S
U  H  T  A  U  C  M  Q  P
Q  A  L  T  S  R  I  Z  L
R  S  L  N  S  B  N  U  M
E  A  Q  A  N  R  G  F  J
U  L  T  S  B  B  T  H  T
Q  O  B  B  L  S  O  H  E
U  A  R  O  W  B  N  G  T
B  L  R  E  B  E  E  J  S
L  R  O  S  W  E  L  L  S
A  L  A  M  A  Z  T  E  C
```

Capital City: Santa Fe

State Bird: Roadrunner

State Tree: Piñon

35

Statehood: 1912

State Flower: Yucca

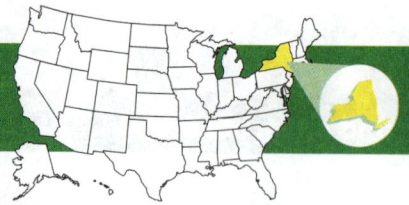

ART PROJECT
Design a postcard for New York City.

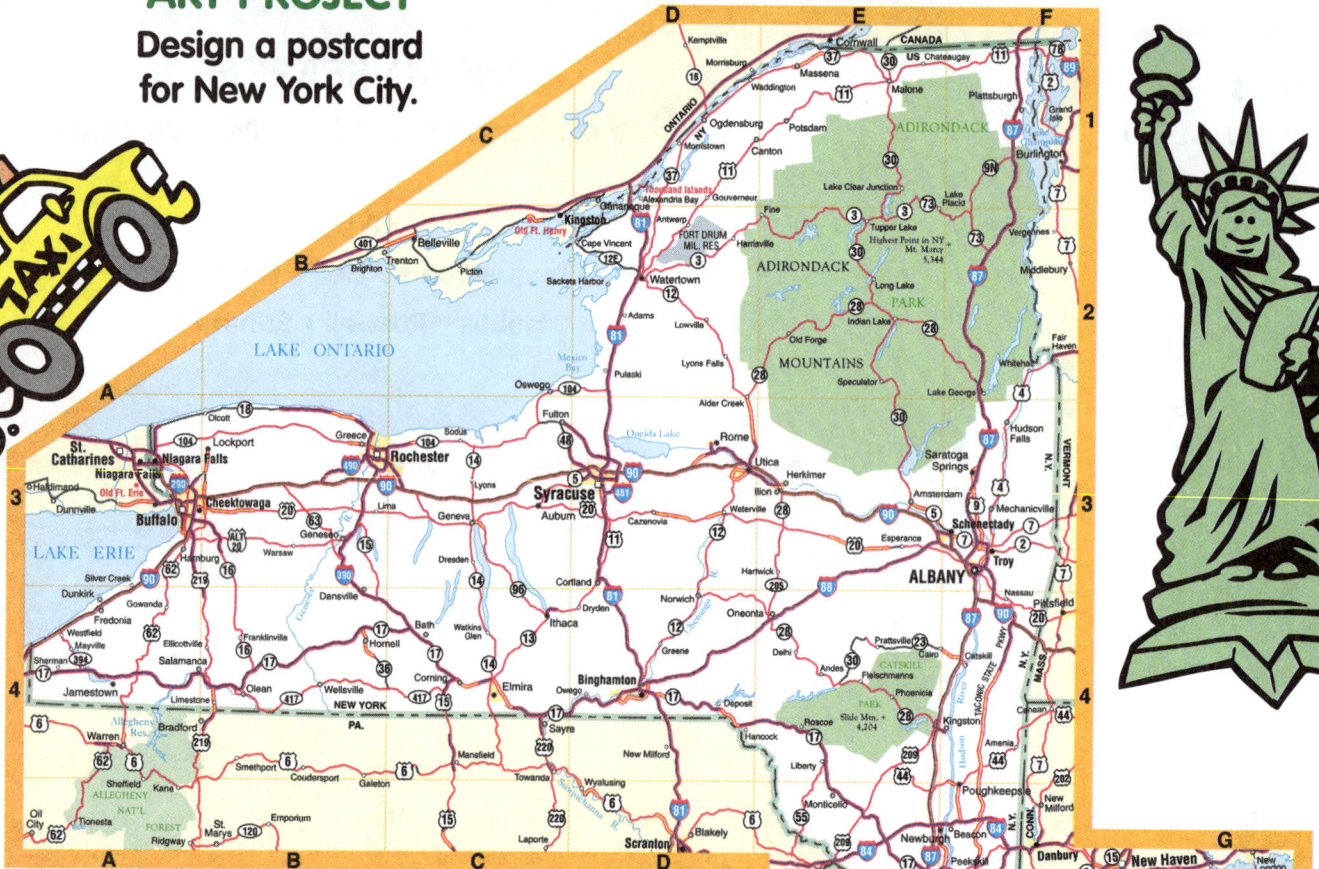

Capital City: Albany
State Bird: Bluebird
State Tree: Sugar Maple
Statehood: 1788
State Flower: Rose

NORTH CAROLINA

Tar Heel State, Old North State

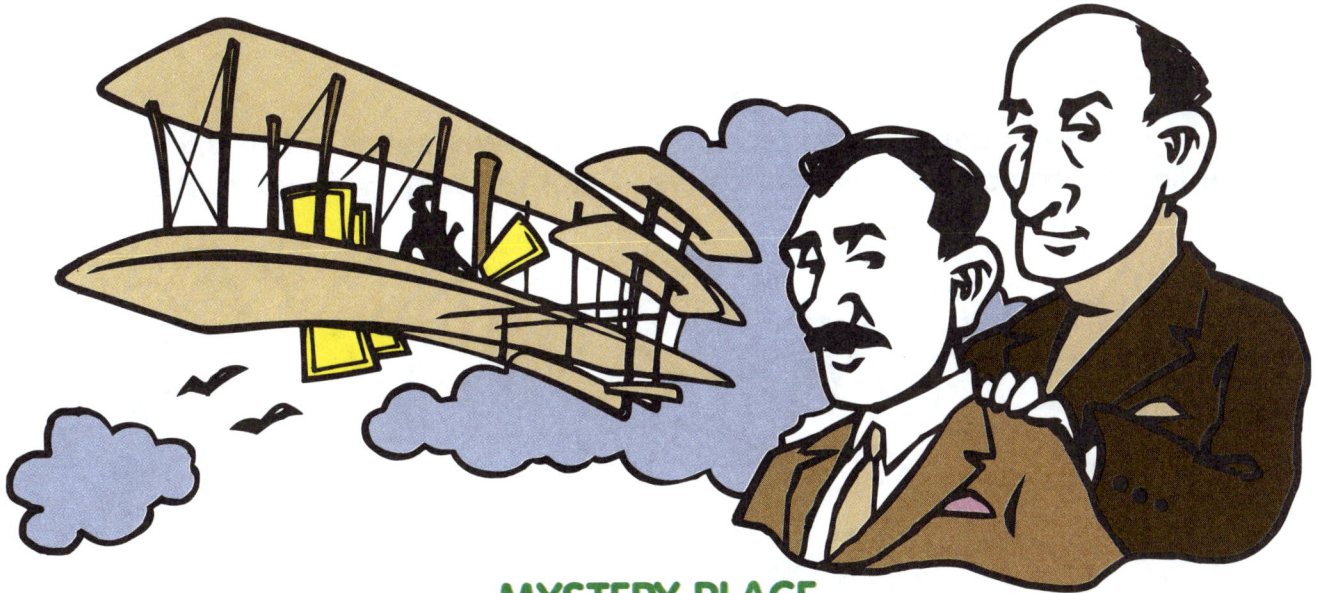

MYSTERY PLACE

Circle all of the letters, except for X's, Z's and O's to spell the site of the Wright Brothers' first airplane flight.

X K O I X Z T X T X O Y Z • O H X X Z A O X W Z O K O

____ ____ ____ ____ • ____ ____ ____ ____

Capital City: Raleigh
State Bird: Cardinal
State Tree: Pine
Statehood: 1789
State Flower: Dogwood

NORTH DAKOTA
Peace Garden State

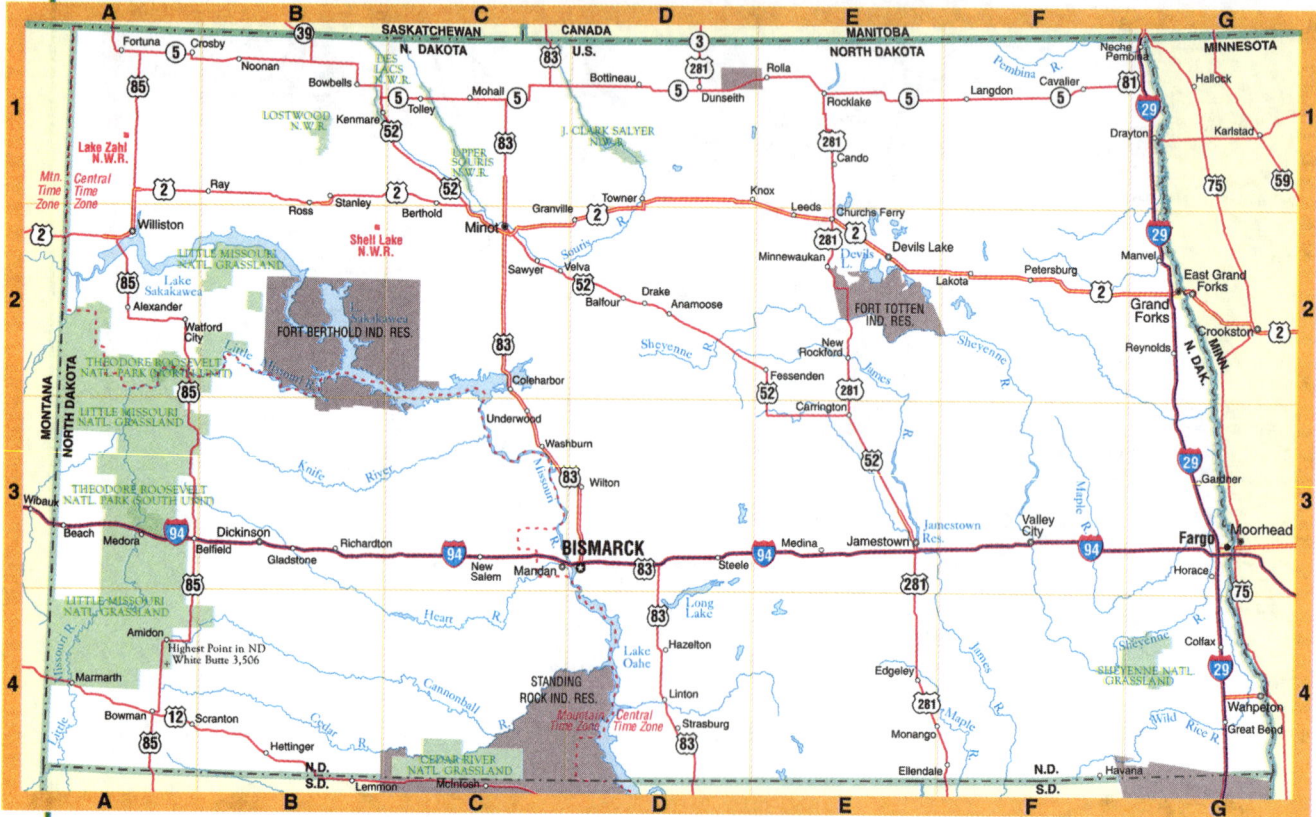

COLORING

North Dakota is the #1 producer of sunflower seeds in the U.S.
Sunflowers come in a variety of colors. Color the page with your favorites!

38

Capital City: Bismarck

State Bird: Western Meadowlark

State Tree: American Elm

Statehood: 1889

State Flower: Wild Prairie Rose

OHIO
Buckeye State

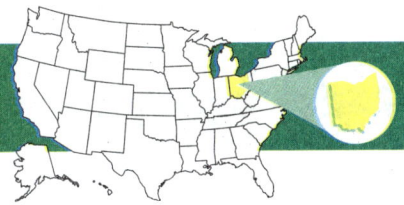

SCRAMBLE

To name this Ohio favorite past time cross out all the capital letters. Write the remaining letters in the spaces.

Map of Ohio showing cities, highways, and Lake Erie.

E f E a E E l l
D f D o o t D b a D l l

_____

_____

39

Capital City: Columbus
State Bird: Cardinal

State Tree: Buckeye

Statehood: 1803
State Flower: Scarlet Carnation

OKLAHOMA
Sooner State

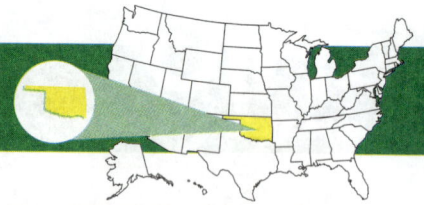

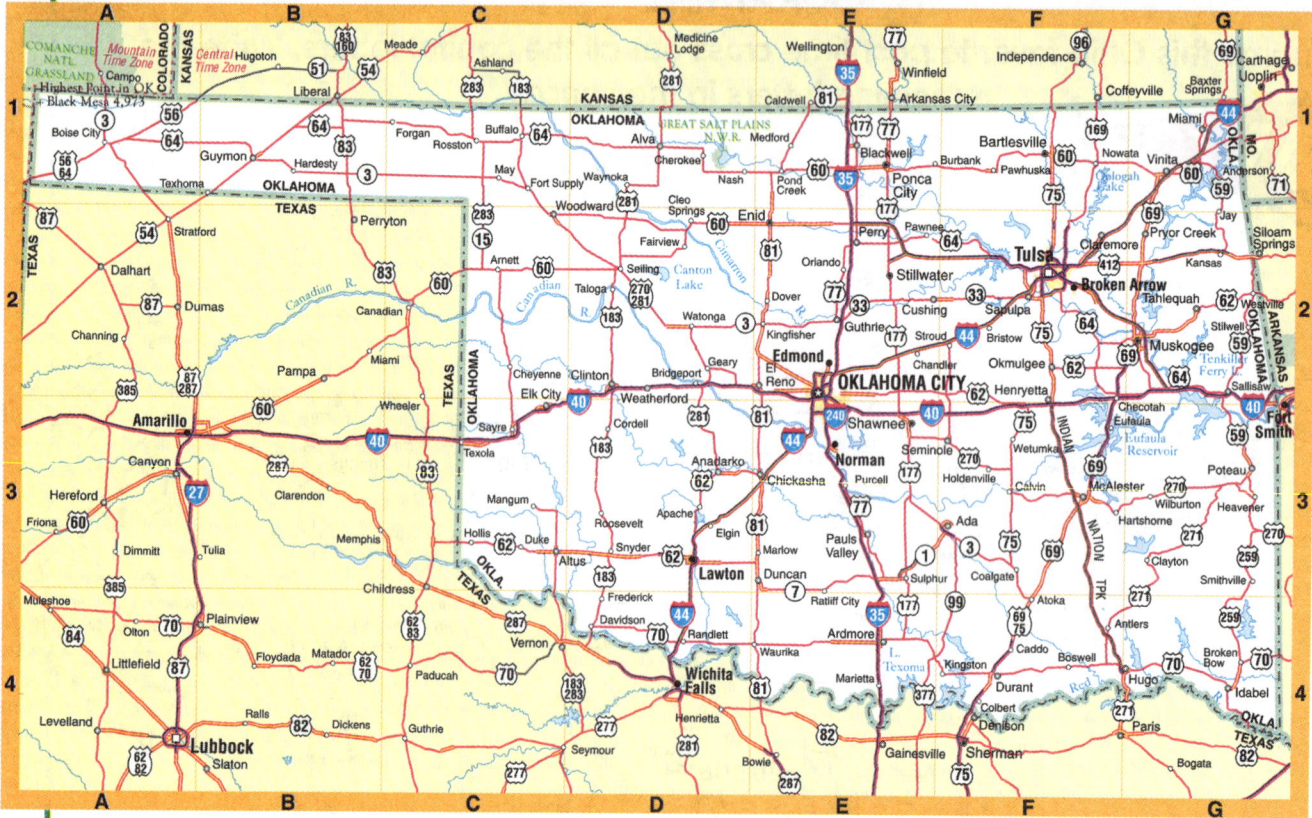

MEMORY GAME
Look at the page for 15 seconds. Turn to page 64 to list all the items you can remember.

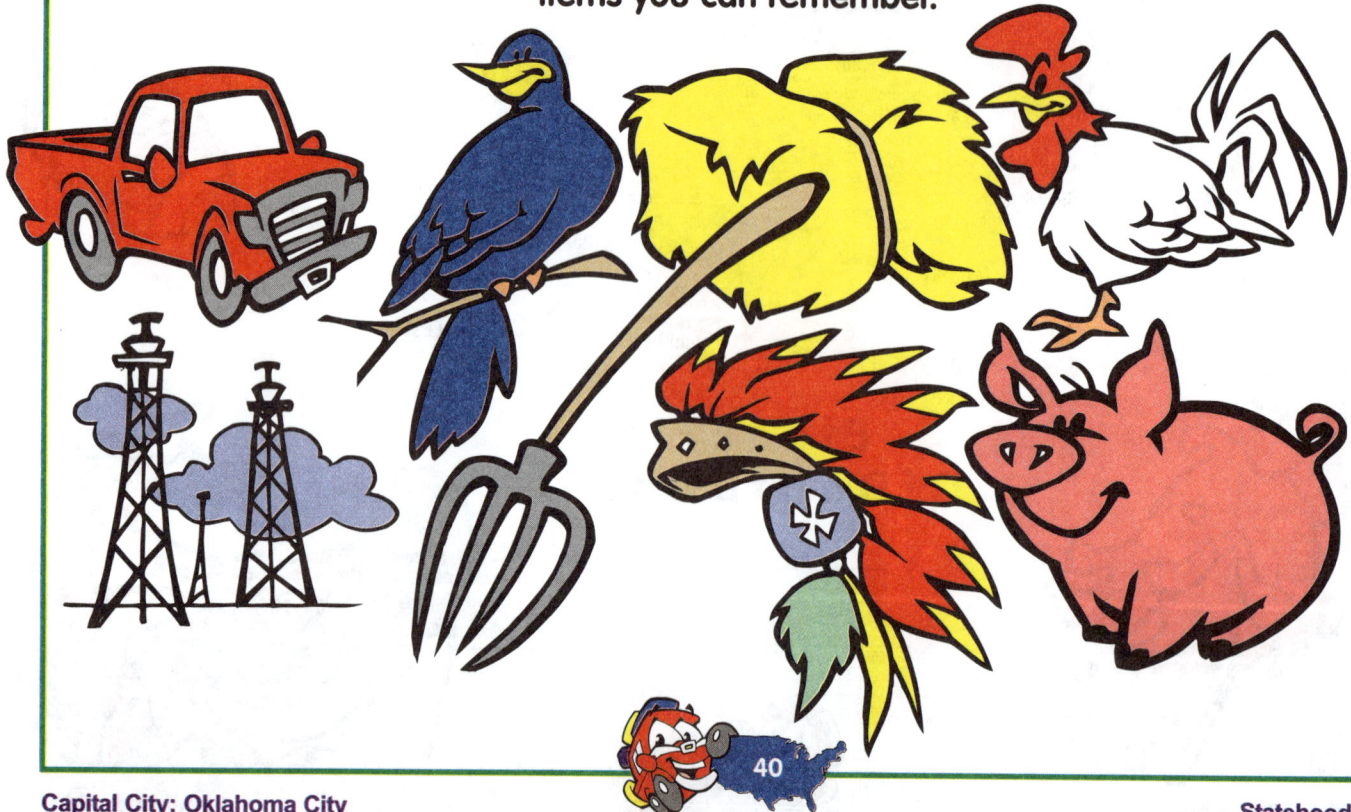

Capital City: Oklahoma City
State Bird: Scissor-tailed Flycatcher

State Tree: Redbud

Statehood: 1907
State Flower: Mistletoe

OREGON

Beaver State

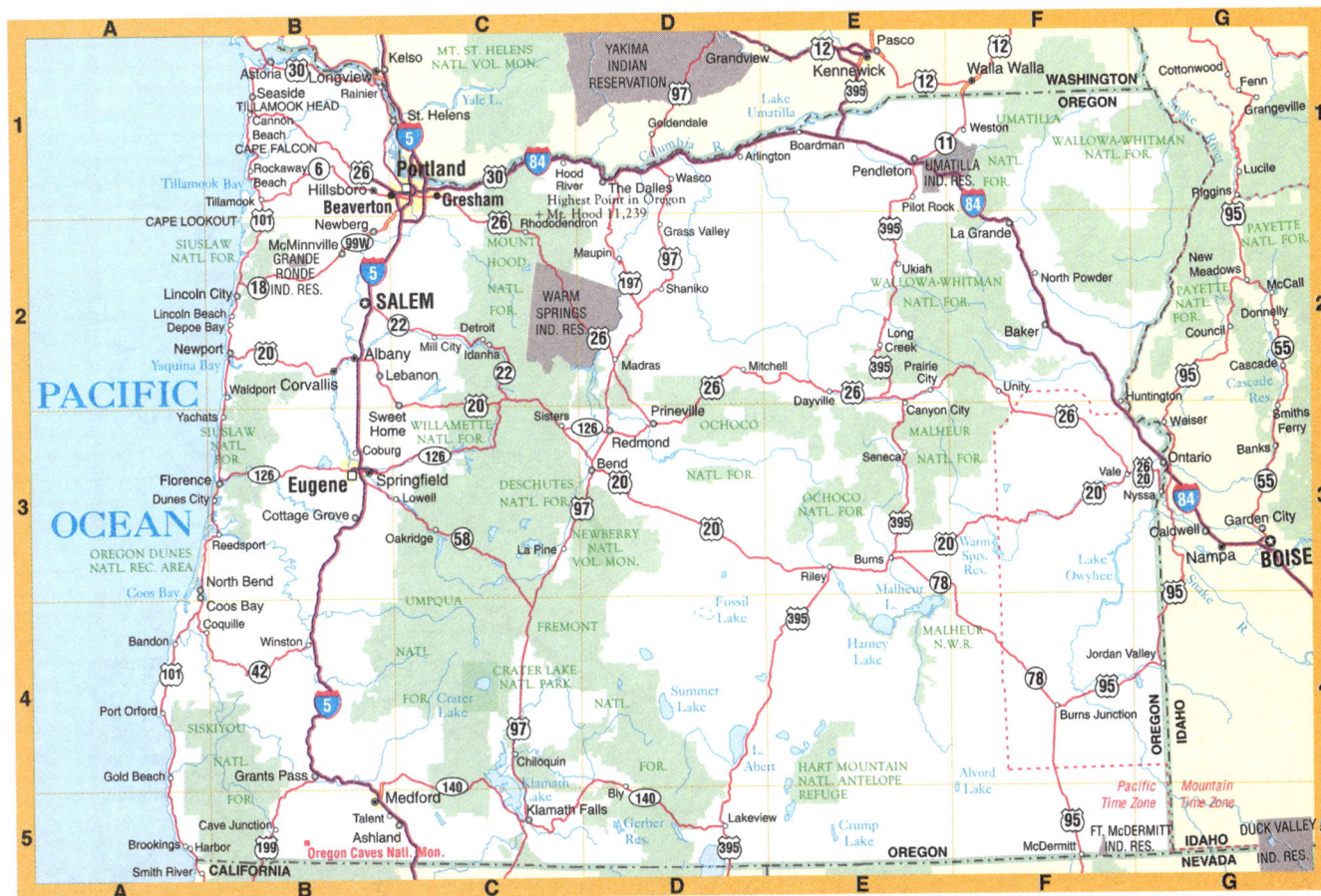

WHAT IS WRONG WITH THIS PICTURE?

Look at this picture closely. Can you find the 10 things that do not belong?

Capital City: Salem
State Bird: Western Meadowlark
State Tree: Douglas Fir
Statehood: 1859
State Flower: Oregon Grape

PENNSYLVANIA
Keystone State

DECODING PUZZLE

Decode the puzzle to name this famous Pennsylvania resident.

○	U	W	X	L
◣	A	P	H	O
▬	E	N	T	B
△	S	Y	I	C

42

Capital City: Harrisburg

State Bird: Ruffed Grouse

State Tree: Hemlock

Statehood: 1787

State Flower: Mountain Laurel

RHODE ISLAND

Little Rhody, Ocean State

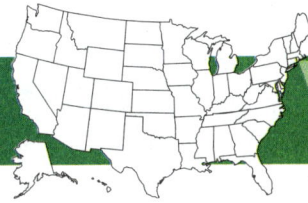

COLOR-BY-NUMBER

#1= Red
#2= Yellow
#3= Purple
#4= Green
#5= Blue
#6= Gray

Capital City: Providence
State Bird: Rhode Island Red

State Tree: Red Maple

Statehood: 1790
State Flower: Violet

43

SOUTH CAROLINA
Palmetto State

WORD SEARCH

South Carolina's other nickname is "Low Country". How many times does "Low Country" appear in this puzzle? Circle each one. It may appear forwards, backwards, up, down and diagonally.

```
C N S U S P S S G U Y R
E L W R I T Q E R P R Y
T O E A N Q L Q L M T R
Z W Y O W C O U N T M T
A C L R S R F E C G U N
T O B I T B R W O F O U
U U Q N N P O C L C O
F N T G L E U L C F W C
B T B Q Q F R O O G O W
S R U O M A U T C B L O
G Y R F P Z L R Q W O L
A R G A E N W L X E O G
L O W C O U N T R Y D L
```

44

Capital City: Columbia
State Bird: Carolina Wren

State Tree: Palmetto

Statehood: 1788
State Flower: Yellow Jessamine

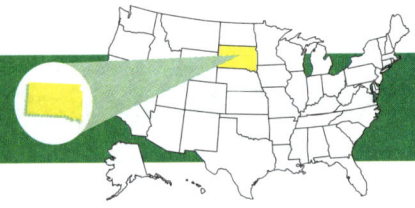

PICTURE PUZZLE

Decode the puzzle to name this famous monument featuring Presidents Roosevelt, Washington, Lincoln and Jefferson.

1=U   2=R   3=M   4=O   5=E   6=S   7=N   8=H   9=T

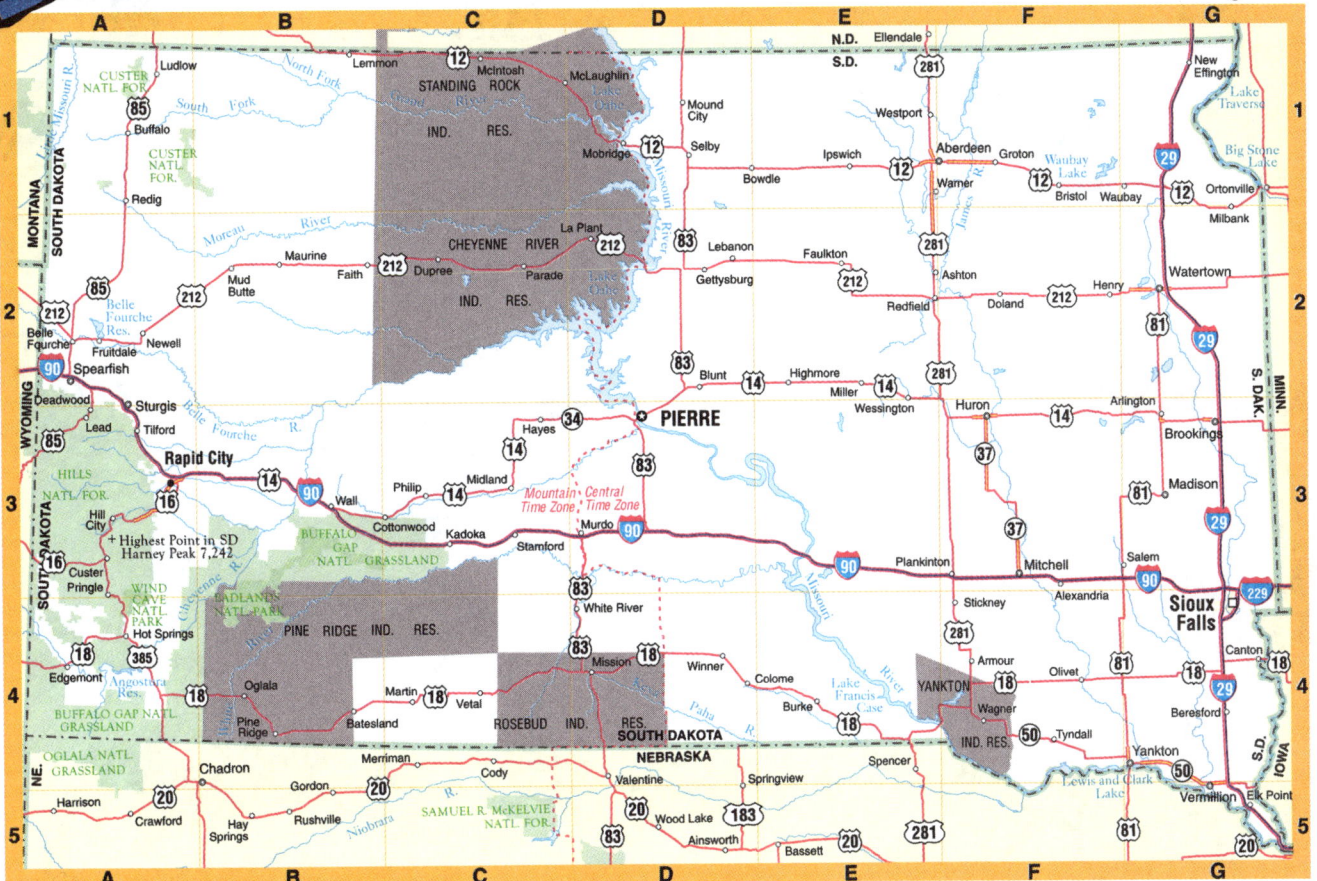

3 4 1 7 9

2 1 6 8 3 4 2 5

45

Capital City: Pierre
State Bird: Chinese Ring-necked Pheasant
State Tree: Black Hills Spruce
Statehood: 1889
State Flower: Pasqueflower

TENNESSEE

Volunteer State

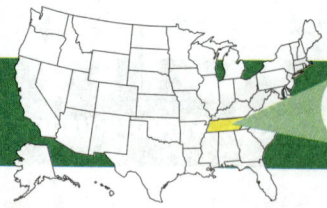

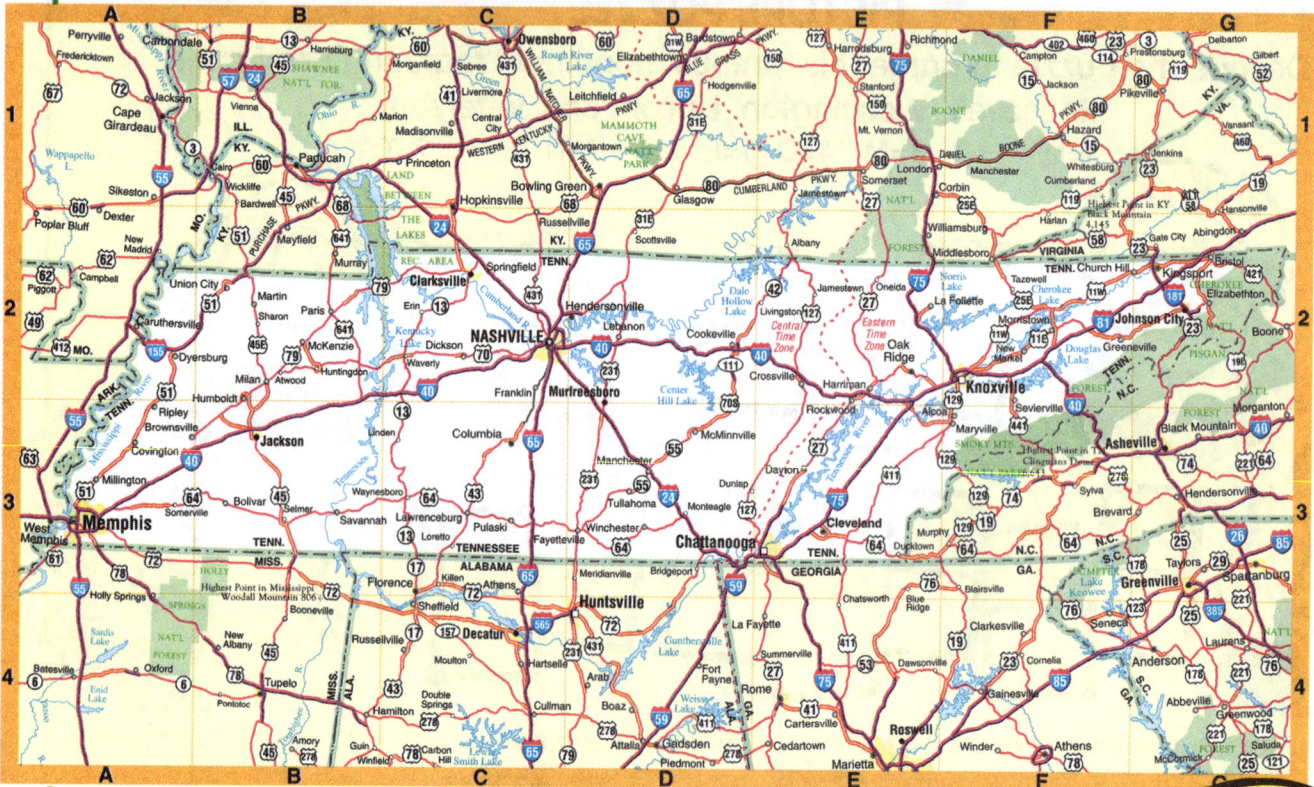

MAZE
Follow the lines to find which instrument Sparky is playing.

46

Capital City: Nashville

State Bird: Mockingbird

State Tree: Tulip Poplar

Statehood: 1796

State Flower: Iris

TEXAS
Lone Star State

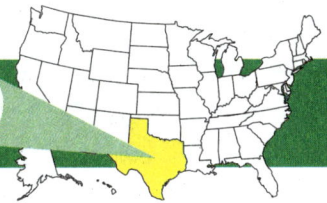

COLORING
Color the animals you would NOT find on a Texas ranch.

Capital City: Austin
State Bird: Mockingbird
State Tree: Pecan
Statehood: 1845
State Flower: Bluebonnet

UTAH
Beehive State

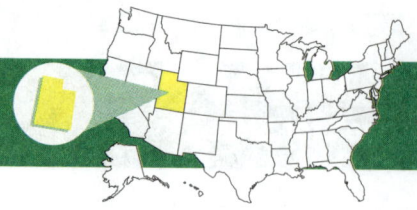

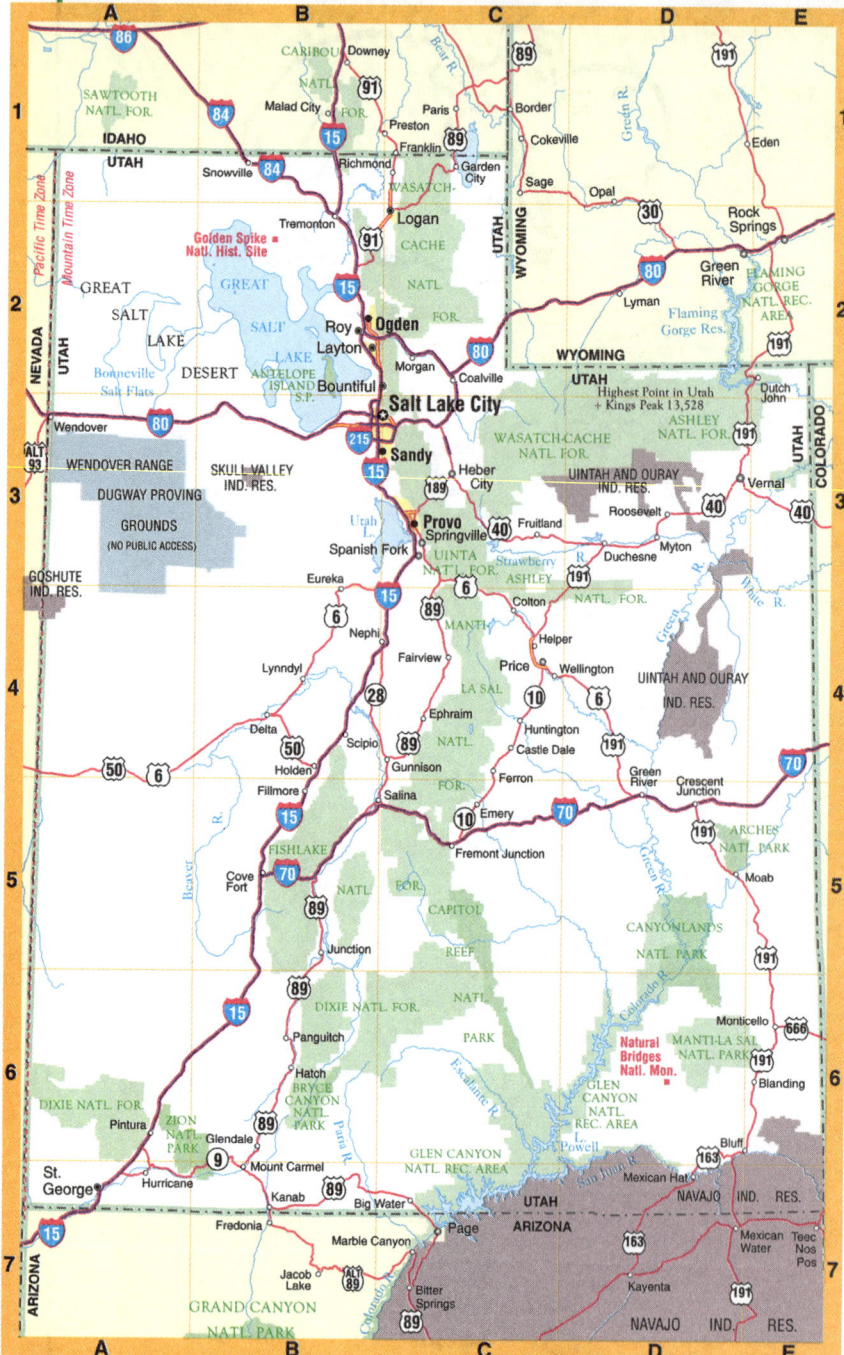

MATCHING

In honor of Utah's state capital, circle all the items that begin with the letter "S".

Capital City: **Salt Lake City**

State Bird: **Seagull**

State Tree: **Blue Spruce**

Statehood: **1896**

State Flower: **Sego Lily**

VERMONT

Green Mountain State

COLOR-BY-NUMBER

Map of Vermont with surrounding region including Canada (Quebec), New York, New Hampshire, Massachusetts. Cities and features labeled:

CANADA / QUEBEC / U.S. / VERMONT

Alburg, Grand Isle, Essex Junction, Burlington, Shelburne, Charlotte, Vergennes, Middlebury, Brandon, Rutland, Whitehall, Wallingford, MONTPELIER, Barre, Marshfield, St. Johnsbury, Woodsville, Woodstock, Ludlow, Chester, Bennington, Wilmington, Brattleboro, Norton, Stewartstown, Colebrook, North Stratford, Lancaster, Littleton, Twin Mountain, Plymouth, Meredith, Hillsboro, Antrim, Manchester, Keene, Peterborough, Troy, Jaffrey, Nashua, Winchenden, Concord

Highest Point in VT Mt. Mansfield 4,393

Lake Champlain, Connecticut River, Green Mountain National Forest, Green Mtns., White Mountain National Forest, Nash Stream State Forest, Saint-Gaudens Natl. Hist. Site

NEW YORK / VERMONT, NEW HAMPSHIRE, MASSACHUSETTS

Color Key

#1= Red	#5= Yellow
#2= Dark Brown	#6= Orange
#3= Green	#7= Light Brown
#4= Black	#8= Blue

49

Capital City: Montpelier

State Bird: Hermit Thrush

State Tree: Sugar Maple

Statehood: 1791

State Flower: Red Clover

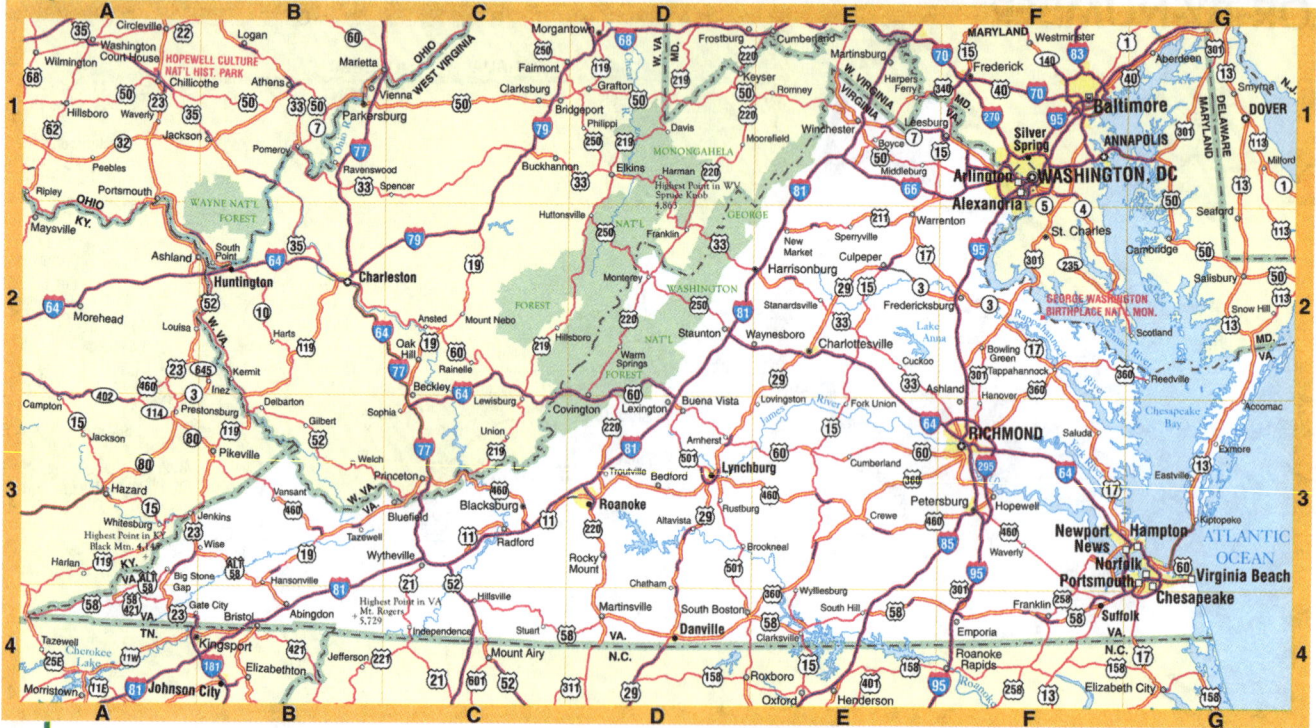

FILL-IN-THE-BLANK

Use the map to complete the sentences below.

#1. Rowanoke is misspelled. Find it in grid [D-3] and spell it correctly _____.

#2. Danville [D-4] is near the _____ border.
Maryland   North Carolina   West Virginia

#3. Richmond [F-3] is the capital city.
True or False

#4. Harrisonburg [E-2] is located at the intersection of U.S. 81 and ____.
250   33   211

#5. Winchester [E-1] is near the _____ border.
Kentucky   Tennessee   West Virginia

#6. The _____ Ocean is on Virginia's eastern border.
Pacific   Atlantic

50

Capital City: Richmond
State Bird: Cardinal

State Tree: Dogwood

Statehood: 1788
State Flower: Dogwood

WASHINGTON

Evergreen State

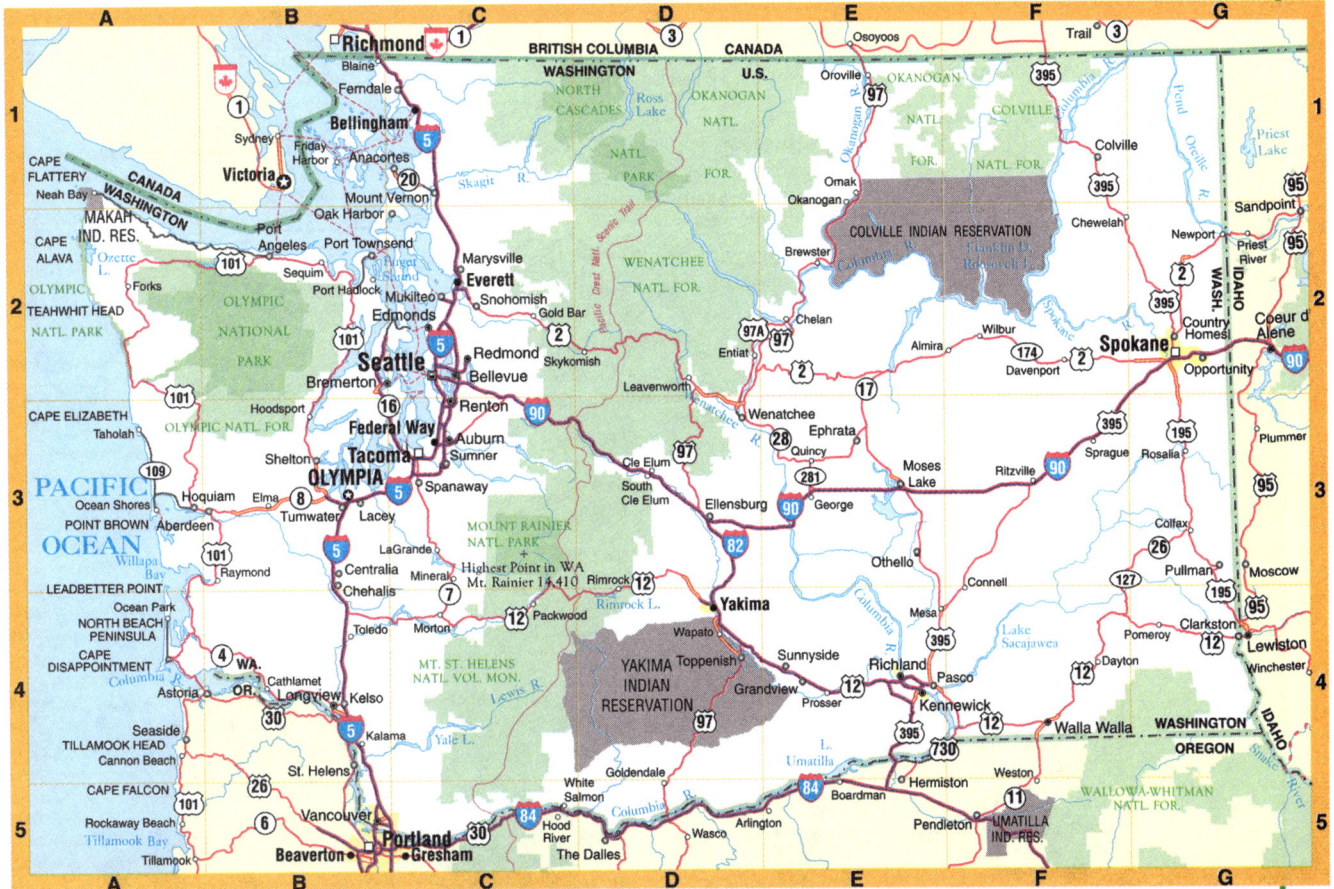

WORD SCRAMBLE

Use the grid coordinates on the map to help you unscramble these Washington cities.

1. I A A Y K M [D-4] _____
2. E A T T S E L [B-2] _____
3. A K N E P O S [G-2] _____
4. T T E E V E R [C-2] _____
5. I Y L A O P M [B-3] _____
6. A A M O C T [C-3] _____

51

Capital City: Olympia

State Bird: Willow Goldfinch

State Tree: Western Hemlock

Statehood: 1889

State Flower: Western Rhododendron

WEST VIRGINIA

Mountain State

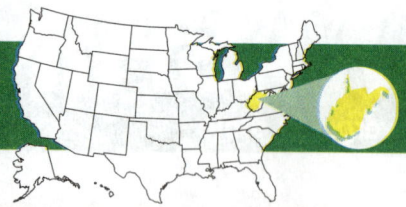

Map of West Virginia and surrounding region with grid coordinates A–F (columns) and 1–6 (rows).

Cities and labels visible on the map include: Galion, Mansfield, Massillon, Canton, East Liverpool, Butler, Kittanning, Mahaffey, State College, Millersburg, Dover, Uhrichsville, Indiana, Altoona, Mount Vernon, Coshocton, Steubenville, Pittsburgh, Johnstown, Cadiz, Washington, Newark, Cambridge, Wheeling, Somerset, Bedford, Chambersburg, Zanesville, Moundsville, Cameron, Morgantown, Cumberland, Somerset, Lancaster, New Martinsville, Martinsburg, Harpers Ferry, Logan, Marietta, Fairmont, Keyser, Romney, Athens, Clarksburg, Grafton, Winchester, Parkersburg, Bridgeport, Moorefield, Boyce, Jackson, Pomeroy, Buckhannon, Philippi, Middleburg, Ravenswood, Elkins, Harman, Point Pleasant, Spencer, Huttonsville, Warrenton, Leon, Franklin, New Market, Culpeper, Sperryville, Ashland, Charleston, Monterey, Harrisonburg, Huntington, Ansted, Mount Nebo, Hillsboro, Staunton, Stanardsville, Charlottesville, Cuckoo, Harts, Oak Hill, Rainelle, Warm Springs, Waynesboro, Fork Union, Kermit, Delbarton, Lewisburg, Covington, Buena Vista, Sophia, Union, Amherst, Cumberland, Gilbert, Welch, Princeton, Bedford, Lynchburg, Pikeville, Vansant, Bluefield, Blacksburg, Roanoke, Rustburg, Crewe, Jenkins, Bland, Radford, Rocky Mount, Altavista, Brookneal, Wytheville

Highest Point in PA Mt. Davis 3,213
Highest Point in WV Spruce Knob 4,863
MONONGAHELA NAT'L FOREST, GEORGE WASHINGTON NAT'L FOREST
WAYNE NAT'L FOREST
Lake Anna, James River

MAZE

Did you know West Virginia is the #1 coal producing state in the U.S. ?

52

Capital City: Charleston
State Bird: Cardinal
State Tree: Sugar Maple
Statehood: 1863
State Flower: Big Rhododendron

WISCONSIN
Badger State

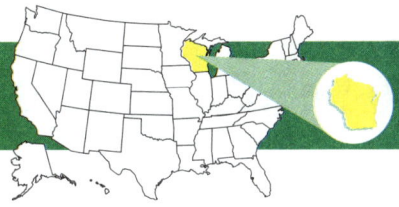

MATCHING
Find the matching cheese wedges.

Capital City: Madison
State Bird: Robin
State Tree: Sugar Maple
Statehood: 1848
State Flower: Wood Violet

WYOMING
Equality State

Map of Wyoming

MONTANA / WYOMING

Beaverhead Natl. For., Mammoth, Tower Junction, Deaver, Bighorn L., Ranchester, Sheridan, Devils Tower Natl. Mon., BLACK HILLS NATL. FOR., 212, 85, 212, Fruitdale, Newell, Spearfish, Sturgis, Island Park, Targhee Natl. For., Cody, 310, 14, Emblem, Banner, BIGHORN NATL. FOR., Buffalo, Gillette, Moorcroft, Sundance, Lead, Tilford, 14, 16, 20, Yellowstone National Park, Shoshone Natl. For., Greybull, 20, Manderson, 90, 16, 14, Upton, Four Corners, Rapid City, Hill City, 16, Ashton, 20, 191, 89, Yellowstone Lake, 16, Worland, 16, Ten Sleep, 87, 25, 16, Newcastle, 85, Custer, 287, Moran, 287, Winchester, Kirby, Kaycee, THUNDER BASIN NATL. GRASSLAND, Riverview, Pringle, Hot Springs, 18, SOUTH DAKOTA, Rigby, Targhee, GRAND TETON NATL. PARK, Jackson Lake, 26, Thermopolis, 789, WIND RIVER, Burris IND. RES., Boysen Res., Shoshoni, Redbird, 85, Edgemont, 385, 18, Idaho Falls, 26, Jackson, BRIDGER-TETON NATL. FOR., Dubois, Crowheart, 26, 20, Moneta, 20, 26, Waltman, Natrona, 25, Lusk, Van Tassell, 18, NEBRASKA, Crawford, 20, Palisades Reservoir, Alpine, 191, 189, Highest Point in Utah Gannett Peak 13,804, Fort Washakie, Riverton, Casper, Douglas, Orin, Glendo, Jay Em, Harrison, Blackfoot Reservoir, Freedom, Thayne, Bondurant, Bull L., 26, Lander, 789, Sweetwater Station, 220, Alcova, MEDICINE BOW NATL. FOR., 26, 85, Soda Springs, Grover, Afton, Daniel, Pinedale, SHOSHONE NATL. FOR., 789, Muddy Gap, Pathfinder Reservoir, Lamont, 287, Seminoe Reservoir, Wheatland, Slater, Torrington, Mitchell, Morrill, 30, Bridger-Teton Natl. For., Border, Cokeville, Farson, Eden, 191, 789, Rawlins, Hanna, Walcott, Elk Mountain, Rock River, 30, Chugwater, 26, 85, Scottsbluff, 385, Montpelier, 91, 89, IDAHO/UTAH, Garden City, Kemmerer, Sage, Opal, 30, Little America, Point of Rocks, 80, 30, Creston Junction, Arlington, Bosler, Meriden, Bayard, 26, Logan, 91, WASATCH-CACHE NATL. FOR., Green River, Rock Springs, 789, Laramie, 25, 85, Evanston, Lyman, FLAMING GORGE NATL. REC. AREA, Flaming Gorge Res., Baggs, CHEYENNE, Pine Bluffs, Kimball, 80, 84, 80, Morgan, WYOMING/UTAH, 191, 287, 30, NEBRASKA, COLORADO

Rocky Mountains, Continental Divide, Green R., Wind R., South Fork, Powder River

PUZZLE-IN-THE-ROUND

Start at C and write every other letter to name these Wyoming cities.

1 _____

2 _____

3 _____

4 _____

5 _____

CCEKCSHOENYLEANRNAEMRIAEWSLUINDSAJNA

54

Capital City: Cheyenne
State Bird: Meadowlark
State Tree: Cottonwood
Statehood: 1890
State Flower: Indian Paintbrush

CANADA

DOT-TO-DOT

Complete the dot-to-dot to see the picture.

MEXICO

WORD SMITH

Using the first letter of these Mexican cities, fill in the boxes.
No word or name can be used twice.

	City Name	Boy's Name	Girl's Name
Acapulco			
Monterrey			
Chihuahua			

INDEX

INDEX TO CITIES, TOWNS & PLACES

ALABAMA
ALABASTER B-3
ALEXANDER CITY D-4
ANDALUSIA C-6
ANNISTON C-3
ARAB C-2
ATHENS B-1
ATMORE B-6
ATTALLA C-2
AUBURN D-4
BAY MINETTE B-7
BESSEMER B-3
BIRMINGHAM B-3
BOAZ C-2
BRANTLEY C-5
BREWTON B-6
BRIDGEPORT D-1
CARBON HILL B-2
CENTRE D-2
CENTREVILLE B-4
CULLMAN C-2
DADEVILLE D-4
DAUPHIN ISLAND A-7
DECATUR B-1
DEMOPOLIS B-4
DOTHAN D-6
DOUBLE SPRINGS B-2
ELBA C-6
ENTERPRISE C-6
EUFAULA D-5
EUTAW A-4
EVERGREEN B-6
FAIRFIELD B-3
FAIRHOPE A-7
FAYETTE A-3
FLORALA C-6
FLORENCE A-1
FORT PAYNE D-2
GADSDEN D-2
GRAND BAY A-7
GREENVILLE C-5
GROVE HILL B-5
GUIN A-2
GUNTERSVILLE C-2
HAMILTON A-2
HARTSELLE B-2
HEFLIN D-3
HUNTSVILLE C-1
JACKSON A-6
JASPER B-2
KILLEN B-1
LAFAYETTE D-4
LANETT D-4
LINDEN B-4
LUVERNE C-5
MADRID D-6
MCINTOSH A-6
MERIDIANVILLE C-1
MIDWAY D-5
MOBILE A-7
MONTGOMERY C-5
MOULTON B-2
MOUNT VERNON A-6
OPELIKA D-4
OPP C-6
OXFORD D-3
OZARK D-6
PHENIX CITY D-4
PIEDMONT D-2
PRATTVILLE C-4
PRICHARD A-7
REFORM A-3
ROANOKE D-3
RUSSELLVILLE A-1
SCOTTSBORO D-1
SELMA B-4
SHEFFIELD B-1
SILAS A-5
SYLACAUGA C-3
TALLADEGA C-3
TROY C-5
TUSCALOOSA A-3
TUSCUMBIA A-1
UNION SPRINGS D-5
UNIONTOWN B-4
WINFIELD A-2

ALASKA
AKUTAN A-5
ALAKANUK A-3
ANCHORAGE C-4
ANVIK B-3
BARROW C-1
BETHEL B-3
CANTWELL C-3
CHIGNIK B-5
COLD BAY A-5
COLLEGE C-3
CORDOVA D-4
DELTA JCT. D-3
DUTCH HARBOR A-5
FAIRBANKS D-3
FORT YUKON D-3
GLENNALLEN D-3
GOODNEWS BAY A-4
HAINES E-4
HOMER C-4
HOUSTON C-3
JUNEAU E-4
KALTAG C-3
KENAI C-4
KETCHIKAN F-5
KODIAK C-4
KOYUK B-2
NAKNEK B-4
NOME B-2
OPHIR C-3
PALMER C-4
PELICAN E-4
POINT HOPE B-1
PRUDHOE BAY D-1
RUBY C-3
SAND POINT B-5
SAVOONGA A-2
SCAMMON BAY A-3
SELAWIK B-2
SELDOVIA C-4
SEWARD D-4
SITKA E-5
SKAGWAY E-4
SLANA D-3
TALKEETNA D-3
TOK D-3
TUNUNAK A-3
UNALAKLEET B-3
VALDEZ D-4
WALES B-2
WHITTIER D-4
WRANGELL F-5
YAKUTAT E-4

ARIZONA
AGUILA B-5
ALPINE E-5
AMADO C-7
APACHE E-7
ASH FORK B-4
BENSON D-6
BISBEE D-7
BITTER SPRINGS C-2
BLACK CANYON CITY C-4
BUCKEYE B-5
BYLAS D-5
CAMERON C-3
CAMP VERDE C-4
CHANDLER B-5
CHINLE D-3
CHINO VALLEY B-4
CONGRESS B-4
DOUGLAS E-7
DUNCAN E-6
EHRENBERG A-5
ELOY C-6
FLAGSTAFF C-4
FLORENCE C-5
FREDONIA B-2
GANADO E-3
GILA BEND B-5
GLENDALE B-5
GLOBE D-5
GRAND CANYON B-2
GUTHRIE E-5
HEBER D-4
HOLBROOK D-4
JACOB LAKE B-2
KAYENTA D-2
KINGMAN A-3
KIRKLAND JCTN. B-4
MARBLE CANYON C-2
MESA C-5
MEXICAN WATER D-2
MIAMI C-5
MOHAWK A-6
MORENCI D-5
NOGALES D-7
ORO VALLEY D-6
PAGE C-2
PAYSON C-4
PHOENIX C-4
PICACHO C-6
PRESCOTT B-4
QUARTZSITE A-5
RYE C-4
SAFFORD D-6
SAN LUIS A-6
SAN SIMON E-6
SANDERS E-3
SELIGMAN B-3
SHOW LOW D-4
SNOWFLAKE D-4
ST. JOHNS D-4
SUN CITY C-5
SUPERIOR C-5
TACNA A-6
TEEC NOS POS E-2
TEMPE C-5
TOMBSTONE D-7
TONALEA C-3
TONOPAH B-5
TOPOCK A-4
TUBA CITY C-3
TUCSON C-6
TUMACACORI C-7
VAIL D-6
WENDEN B-5
WICKENBURG B-5
WIKIEUP B-4
WILLCOX D-6
WILLIAMS C-3
WINSLOW C-4
YUCCA A-6
YUMA A-6

ARKANSAS
ALMA A-2
ARKADELPHIA C-4
ASH FLAT D-2
BALD KNOB D-3
BATESVILLE D-2
BENTON C-3
BERRYVILLE B-1
BRINKLEY E-3
CAMDEN B-5
CLARENDON D-4
CLARKSVILLE B-2
CLINTON C-2
CONWAY C-2
CORNING E-1
CROSSETT D-6
DARDANELLE B-3
DE QUEEN A-4
DERMOTT D-5
DUMAS D-5
EL DORADO C-6
ENGLAND D-4
EUREKA SPRINGS B-1
FAYETTEVILLE A-2
FORDYCE C-5
FOREST CITY E-3
FORT SMITH A-3
FULTON A-5
GLENWOOD B-4
HAMBURG D-6
HARDY D-2
HARRISON B-2
HEBER SPRINGS D-3
HELENA E-4
HOT SPRINGS B-4
HUGHES E-3
IMBODEN D-2
JACKSONVILLE D-3
JONESBORO E-2
JUNCTION CITY B-6
LAKE VILLAGE D-5
LEWISVILLE A-5
LITTLE ROCK B-3
MAGNOLIA B-6
MALVERN C-4
MANSFIELD A-3
MARIANNA E-4
MARKED TREE E-3
MARSHALL C-2
MCCRORY D-3
MCGEHEE D-5
MENA A-4
MONTICELLO D-5
MONTROSE D-6
MORRILTON B-3
MOUNT IDA B-4
MOUNTAIN HOME C-1
NEWPORT D-2
N. LITTLE ROCK C-2
OLA B-3
PARAGOULD E-2
PELSOR C-2
PIGGOTT E-1
PINE BLUFF C-4
POCAHONTAS D-1
PRESCOTT B-5
ROGERS A-1
RUSSELLVILLE B-3
SEARCY D-3
SHERIDAN C-4
SILOAM SPRINGS A-1
SPRINGDALE A-2
STAR CITY D-5
STUTTGART D-4
TEXARKANA A-6
VAN BUREN A-3
WALDO B-5
WALDRON A-4
WALNUT RIDGE E-2
WEST MEMPHIS E-3
WYNNE E-3
YELLVILLE C-2

CALIFORNIA
ADIN C-1
ALTURAS C-1
ANAHEIM D-6
ARCATA A-1
AUBURN C-3
AVALON D-7
BAKER E-5
BAKERSFIELD D-5
BARSTOW E-5
BELDEN B-2
BENTON D-4
BERKELEY B-3
BIEBER C-1
BIG SUR B-5
BISHOP D-4
BLACKWELLS CORNER C-5
BLAIRSDEN C-2
BLYTHE F-6
BRADLEY C-5
BRAWLEY F-7
BRIDGEPORT C-3
BURNEY B-1
CALEXICO F-7
CAMBRIA B-5
CANBY C-1
CANTIL D-5
CHICO B-2
CHULA VISTA D-7
COACHELLA E-6
CORNING B-2
CRESCENT CITY A-1
DAVIS CREEK C-1
DELANO D-5
DESERT CENTER F-6
DORRIS B-1
DOYLE C-2
DUNSMUIR B-1
EL CAJON D-7
EL CENTRO E-7
ESCONDIDO E-7
EUREKA A-1
EXETER D-5
FORTUNA A-2
FOUR CORNERS C-5
FRESNO C-4
GAVIOTA C-6
GILROY B-4
GRASS VALLEY B-3
GREENFIELD B-4
GRIDLEY B-2
HANFORD C-5
HAYWARD B-4
HOLLISTER B-4
HUNTINGTON BCH. D-6
INDEPENDENCE D-4
INGLEWOOD D-6
JACKSON B-3
KING CITY B-4
KLAMATH A-1
LAKESIDE E-7
LANCASTER D-6
LEE VINING D-3
LIKELY C-1
LODI B-3
LOLETA A-2
LOMPOC C-6
LONE PINE D-4
LONG BEACH D-6
LOS ANGELES D-6
LOS BANOS C-4
LOS MOLINOS B-2
LOS OLIVOS C-6
LUCIA B-5
LUDLOW E-6
MADERA C-4
MANTECA B-4
MARIPOSA C-4
MARYSVILLE B-3
MCKINLEYVILLE A-1
MERCED C-4
MODESTO C-4
MOJAVE D-5
MONTEREY B-4
MORRO BAY B-5
NAPA B-3
NEEDLES F-5
NICE B-3
OAKLAND B-4
OCEANSIDE D-7
OLANCHA D-5
ONTARIO D-6
ORICK A-1
ORLAND B-2
OROVILLE B-2
OXNARD D-6
PACIFICA A-4
PALM SPRINGS E-6
PASADENA D-6
PETALUMA A-3
PISMO BEACH B-5
PLACERVILLE C-3
POMONA D-6
QUINCY B-2
RED BLUFF B-2
REDDING B-2
REDWAY A-2
RICHMOND B-3
RIDGECREST D-5
RIVERSIDE E-6
ROSEVILLE B-3
SACRAMENTO B-3
SALINAS B-4
SAN BERNARDINO E-6
SAN DIEGO D-7
SAN FRANCISCO A-4
SAN JOSE B-4
SAN LUIS OBISPO C-5
SAN MATEO A-4
SAN RAFAEL A-3
SAN SIMEON B-5
SANGER C-4
SANTA ANA D-6
SANTA BARBARA C-6
SANTA CRUZ B-4
SANTA MARIA C-6
SANTA ROSA A-3
SELMA C-4
SHASTA LAKE B-2
SMITH RIVER A-1
SONORA C-3
STOCKTON B-4
SUNNYVALE B-4
SUSANVILLE C-2
TEHACHAPI D-5
TEMECULA E-7
TERMO C-1
THOUSAND OAKS C-6
TRACY B-4
TULARE C-5
TURLOCK B-4
UKIAH A-3
VALLEJO B-3
VENTURA C-6
VICTORVILLE E-6
VISALIA C-5
WASCO C-5
WATSONVILLE B-4
WEAVERVILLE A-1
WEED B-1
WILLIAMS B-3
WILLITS A-2
WILLOWS B-2
WOODLAND B-3
YREKA B-1
YUBA CITY B-3
YUCCA VALLEY E-6

COLORADO
AKRON F-1
ALAMOSA D-4
ANTON F-2
ANTONITO D-5
ARVADA D-2
AULT E-1
AURORA E-2
BLANCA D-5
BOULDER D-2
BRIGHTON E-2
BURLINGTON F-2
CAMPO G-5
CANON CITY D-3
CHEYENNE WELLS F-3
CLIFTON B-3
COLORADO SPRNGS.E-3
COPE F-2
CORTEZ A-4
CRAIG B-1
DE BEQUE B-2
DEL NORTE C-4
DELTA B-3
DENVER E-2
DINOSAUR A-1
DOVE CREEK A-4
DURANGO B-5
EADS F-3
EMPIRE D-2
EVANS E-1
FAIRPLAY D-3
FORT COLLINS D-1
FORT LUPTON E-1
FORT MORGAN E-2
FOWLER E-4
FRISCO D-2
FRUITA A-3
GLENWOOD SPRGS. C-2
GRANBY D-2
GRAND JUNCTION A-3
GREELEY E-1
GUNNISON C-3
GYPSUM C-2
HAXTUN F-1
HAYDEN C-1
HOLLY G-4
HOLYOKE F-1
HUGO F-3
IDALIA G-2
KIT CARSON F-3
KREMMLING C-2
LA JARA D-5
LA JUNTA F-4
LAKEWOOD D-2
LAMAR G-4
LAST CHANCE F-2
LEADVILLE C-2
LIMON F-3
LITTLETON E-2
LONGMONT D-1
LOVELAND D-1
MANCOS B-4
MEEKER B-2
MINTURN C-2
MONTE VISTA D-4
MONTROSE B-3
NEW CASTLE B-2
OLATHE B-3
OURAY B-4
PAGOSA SPRINGS C-5
PUEBLO E-3
RAMAH E-3
RIDGWAY B-2
RIFLE B-2
SAGUACHE C-4
SALIDA D-3
SILVERTON B-4
SIMLA E-3
SPRINGFIELD G-4
STEAMBOAT SPRS. C-1
STERLING F-1
THORNTON E-2
TRINIDAD E-5
WALSENBURG E-4
WIGGINS E-2
WINTER PARK D-2
YUMA F-2

CONNECTICUT
ANDOVER D-2
ANSONIA B-3
ASHFORD E-2
AVON C-2
BRIDGEPORT B-4
BRISTOL C-3
BROOKFIELD B-3
CANAAN B-1
CHESTER D-3
COLCHESTER D-3
DANBURY A-3
ENFIELD C-2
FAIRFIELD B-4
GRANBY C-1
GREENWICH A-5
GROTON E-4
HAMDEN C-3
HAMPTON E-2
HARTFORD D-2
HEBRON D-3
KENT A-2
LITCHFIELD B-2
MANCHESTER D-2
MARLBOROUGH D-3
MERIDEN C-3
MIDDLETOWN C-3
MILFORD B-4
MYSTIC E-4
NAUGATUCK C-3
NEW BRITAIN C-3
NEW HARTFORD B-2
NEW HAVEN C-4
NEW LONDON E-4
NEW MILFORD B-3
NORFOLK B-1
NORWALK B-4
NORWICH E-3
PUTNAM E-2
SHELTON B-4
SIMSBURY C-2
STAMFORD A-5
THOMASTON B-2
THOMPSON E-1
TORRINGTON B-2
TRUMBULL B-4
UNION E-1
WALLINGFORD C-3
WATERBURY C-3
WEST HAVEN C-4
WILTON A-4
WINSTED B-2

DELAWARE
BETHANY BEACH D-6
BOWERS BEACH C-4
BRIDGEVILLE B-5
DOVER C-4
GEORGETOWN C-5
LAUREL B-6
LEWES C-5
MIDDLETOWN B-3
MILFORD C-5
MILLSBORO C-6
NEW CASTLE B-2
NEWARK A-2
SEAFORD B-6
SMYRNA B-3
WILMINGTON B-1

FLORIDA
ALVA F-5
APALACHICOLA C-2
ARCADIA F-5
ASTOR F-3
AVON PARK F-4
BALDWIN E-2
BAYONET POINT E-3
BELLE GLADE G-5
BONITA SPRINGS F-5
BRADENTON E-4
BROOKSVILLE E-3
BUNNELL F-2
CAPE CANAVERAL G-3
CAPE CORAL E-5
CARRABELLE C-2
CEDAR KEY D-3
CHIEFLAND E-3
CLEARWATER E-4
CLERMONT F-3
CLEWISTON G-5
COCOA G-3
CORAL GABLES G-6
CORAL SPRINGS G-5
CRAWFORDVILLE C-2
CRESCENT BEACH F-2
CRESTVIEW B-1
CRYSTAL RIVER E-3
DAYTONA BEACH G-3
DE LAND F-3
DEFUNIAK SPRINGS B-1
DELTONA F-3
DUNEDIN E-4
EASTPOINT C-2
EDGEWATER G-3
ENGLEWOOD E-5
FERNANDINA BEACH F-1
FLAGLER BEACH F-2
FORT LAUDERDALE G-6
FORT MYERS F-5
FORT PIERCE G-4
FORT WALTON BCH. B-1
GAINESVILLE E-2
GOLDEN GATE F-6
GREEN COVE SPGS. F-2
HAINES CITY F-4
HAWTHORNE F-2
HIGH SPRINGS E-2
HOLLYWOOD G-6
HOMESTEAD G-6
HOMOSASSA SPRGS.D-3
JACKSONVILLE F-1
JACKSONVILLE BCH. F-2
JUPITER G-5
KEY LARGO G-7
KEY WEST F-7
KISSIMMEE F-4
LAKE BUTLER E-2
LAKE CITY E-2
LAKE WORTH G-5
LAKELAND E-4
LARGO E-4
LEESBURG F-3
LIVE OAK E-2
LUTZ E-4
LYNN HAVEN B-1
MARATHON F-7
MARCO F-6
MARIANNA C-1
MAYO D-2
MELBOURNE G-4
MERRITT ISLAND G-3
MIAMI G-6
MILTON A-1
MIMS G-3
MONTICELLO D-1
NAPLES F-6
NEW PORT RICHEY D-4
NEW SMYRNA BCH. G-3
OCALA E-3
OKEECHOBEE F-5
ORLANDO F-3
ORMOND BEACH G-2
PALATKA F-2
PALM BAY G-4
PALM COAST F-2
PANAMA CITY B-2
PENSACOLA A-1
PERRINE G-6
PERRY D-2
PORT CHARLOTTE F-5
PORT ORANGE G-3
PORT ST. LUCIE G-5
PORT ST. JOE B-2
PUNTA GORDA F-5
QUINCY C-1
SANFORD F-3
SANIBEL E-5
SARASOTA E-4
SEBASTIAN G-4
SEBRING F-4
SPRING HILL E-3
SPRINGFIELD B-2
ST. AUGUSTINE F-2
ST. CLOUD F-4
ST. PETERSBURG D-4
STARKE E-2
STUART G-5
TALLAHASSEE D-1
TAMPA E-4
TITUSVILLE G-3
VENICE E-5
VERO BEACH G-4
WALDO E-2
WEST PALM BEACH G-5
WILDWOOD F-3
WINTER HAVEN F-4
YULEE F-1

GEORGIA

ABBEVILLE C-4
ALAPAHA C-5
ALBANY B-5
ALMA C-5
AMERICUS B-4
ATHENS C-2
ATLANTA B-2
AUGUSTA D-3
BAINBRIDGE B-5
BAXLEY D-4
BLAIRSVILLE B-1
BLUE RIDGE B-1
BREMEN A-2
BRUNSWICK D-5
CAIRO B-6
CAMILLA B-5
CARROLLTON A-3
CARTERSVILLE A-2
CEDARTOWN A-2
CHATSWORTH A-1
CLARKESVILLE B-1
CLAXTON D-4
COLQUITT A-5
COLUMBUS A-4
CORDELE B-4
CORNELIA B-2
COVINGTON B-3
CUTHBERT A-4
DARIEN D-5
DAWSON B-5
DAWSONVILLE B-2
DONALSONVILLE . . . A-5
DOUGLAS C-5
DUBLIN C-4
EAST POINT A-2
EASTMAN C-4
EATONTON C-3
ELLAVILLE B-4
FOLKSTON D-6
GAINESVILLE B-2
GEORGETOWN A-4
GLENVILLE D-4
GRIFFIN B-3
HAZLEHURST C-4
HOMERVILLE C-5
JESUP D-5
KINGSLAND D-6
LA FAYETTE A-1
LA GRANGE A-3
LOUISVILLE C-3
LUDOWICI D-5
LYONS D-4
MACON B-3
MADISON C-3
MARIETTA A-2
MCRAE C-4
MILLEDGEVILLE C-3
MOULTRIE B-5
NAHUNTA D-5
PATTERSON D-5
PEARSON C-5
PERRY B-4
QUITMAN B-6
RICHLAND A-4
ROBERTA B-4
ROME A-2
ROSWELL B-2
SAVANNAH D-4
SPARTA C-3
STATESBORO D-4
SUMMERVILLE A-2
SWAINSBORO D-4
SYLVESTER B-5
TALBOTTON A-3
THOMASTON A-3
THOMASVILLE B-6
THOMSON C-3
TIFTON C-5
VALDOSTA C-6
VIDALIA C-4
WARNER ROBINS . . . B-4
WASHINGTON C-3
WAYCROSS D-5
WAYNESBORO D-3
WINDER B-2
WRENS C-3

HAWAII

CAPTAIN COOK . . . E-4
HAENA A-1
HALAWA E-2
HANA F-3
HILO G-4
HONOKAA F-3
HONOKOHAU E-2
HONOLULU C-2
KAILUA D-2
KAILUA-KONA E-4
KAPAA B-1
KAPOHO G-4
KAUNAKAKAI D-2
KAWAIHAE E-3
KEAAU G-4
KEKAHA A-1
KEOKEA F-4
KIHEI E-3
KILAUEA B-1
LAHAINA E-2
LAIE C-1
LANAI CITY D-2
LAUPAHOEHOE . . . G-3
LIHUE B-1
MAUNALOA D-2
NAALEHU F-5
NANAKULI C-2
PAHALA F-4
PAPA F-4
ULUPALAKUA E-3
VOLCANO G-4
WAIANAE C-2
WAIMEA F-3

IDAHO

AMERICAN FALLS . . C-6
ARCO C-6
ASHTON E-5
ATOMIC CITY C-6
BANKS A-5
BELLEVUE C-6
BLACKFOOT D-6
BLISS B-6
BOISE A-6
BONNERS FERRY . . A-1
BURLEY C-7
CALDWELL A-6
CAMBRIDGE A-5
CAREY C-6
CARMEN C-4
CASCADE A-5
CHALLIS B-5
COEUR D'ALENE . . . A-2
COTTONWOOD A-3
COUNCIL A-5
DONNELLY A-5
DOWNEY D-7
DUBOIS D-5
EASTPORT A-1
ELLIS C-5
FAIRFIELD B-6
FENN A-4
FRANKLIN D-7
GARDEN CITY A-6
GEORGETOWN E-7
GLENNS FERRY . . . B-6
GOODING B-6
GRANGEVILLE A-4
GREER A-3
HAILEY C-6
HILL CITY B-6
HOLLISTER B-7
IDAHO FALLS D-6
ISLAND PARK E-5
JEROME B-7
KAMIAH B-3
KELLOGG A-2
KETCHUM B-6
KOOSKIA A-3
LAKEVIEW A-2
LEWISTON A-3
LOWELL A-3
LUCILE A-4
MACKAY C-5
MALAD CITY D-7
MCCALL A-5

ILLINOIS

ALTON B-5
ARCOLA D-4
AURORA D-2
BARTONVILLE B-3
BEARDSTOWN B-4
BELLEVILLE B-5
BELVIDERE C-1
BLOOMINGTON C-3
CAIRO C-7
CAMP POINT A-4
CARBONDALE C-7
CARMI D-6
CENTRALIA C-6
CHAMPAIGN D-4
CHENOA C-3
CHESTER B-6
CHICAGO D-2
CHRISMAN D-4
CLINTON C-4
COLLINSVILLE B-5
DANVILLE D-4
DE KALB C-1
DECATUR C-4
DIXON C-2
DU QUOIN C-6
EFFINGHAM D-5
ELGIN D-1
EUREKA B-3
EVANSTON D-1
FLORA D-5
GALENA B-1
GALESBURG B-3
HAMILTON A-3
HARRISBURG D-7
HAVANA B-3
HEYWORTH C-3
JACKSONVILLE B-4
JOLIET D-2
KANKAKEE D-2
KEWANEE B-3
LA SALLE C-2
LAWRENCEVILLE . . . D-5
LEWISTOWN B-3
LEXINGTON C-3
LINCOLN C-4
MENDOTA C-2
MILFORD D-3
MOLINE B-2
MONMOUTH B-3
MONTICELLO D-4

INDIANA

ALEXANDRIA C-3
ANDERSON C-3
ANGOLA D-1
ATTICA B-3
AUBURN D-1
AURORA D-5
BEDFORD C-6
BICKNELL B-6
BLOOMINGTON C-5
BROWNSBURG B-4
BROWNSTOWN C-5
CHURUBUSCO D-2
COLUMBIA CITY C-2
COLUMBUS C-5
CRAWFORDSVILLE . . B-4
DALE B-7
DECATUR D-2
DELPHI B-3
ELKHART C-1
EVANSVILLE A-7
FORT WAYNE D-2
FRANKFORT C-3
FRANKLIN C-4
GARY B-1
GOSHEN C-1
GREENCASTLE B-4
GREENFIELD C-4
GREENSBURG D-5
HUNTINGBURG B-6
HUNTINGTON C-2
INDIANAPOLIS B-4
JASPER B-6
JEFFERSONVILLE . . . D-6
KENDALLVILLE D-1
KENTLAND B-2
KNIGHTSTOWN D-4
KNOX C-2
KOKOMO C-3
LA PORTE B-1
LAFAYETTE B-3
LAGRANGE D-1
LEBANON B-4
LIBERTY D-4
LOGANSPORT B-2
LOOGOOTEE B-6
LYNN D-3
MADISON D-6
MARION C-2
MEDARYVILLE B-2
MICHIGAN CITY B-1

IOWA

ALGONA C-1
AMES D-3
ATLANTIC C-3
BLOOMFIELD E-4
BURLINGTON F-4
CARROLL C-2
CASCADE F-2
CEDAR FALLS E-2
CEDAR RAPIDS F-3
CHARITON D-4
CHARLES CITY E-1
CHEROKEE B-2
CLARINDA B-4
CLINTON G-3
CORNING C-4
COUNCIL BLUFFS . . . B-4
CRESTON C-4
DAVENPORT F-3
DECORAH F-1
DENISON B-3
DES MOINES D-3
DUBUQUE F-2
DYERSVILLE F-2
FAIRFIELD E-4
FORT DODGE C-2
FORT MADISON F-4
GARNER D-1
GLENWOOD B-4
GUTTENBERG F-2
HARLAN B-3
HOLSTEIN B-2
HUMBOLDT C-2
INDEPENDENCE E-2
INDIANOLA D-3
IOWA CITY F-3
IOWA FALLS D-2
KEOKUK F-4
LE MARS B-2
MAQUOKETA F-2
MASON CITY D-1
MISSOURI VALLEY . . B-3
MONTEZUMA E-3
MONTICELLO F-2
MOUNT AYR C-4
MOUNT PLEASANT . . F-4
MUSCATINE F-3
NASHUA E-1
NEW HAMPTON E-1
NEW LONDON F-4
NEW SHARON E-3
NEWTON D-3
OAKLAND B-3

MCCAMMON D-7
MIDVALE A-5
MONTPELIER E-7
MOORE C-6
MOSCOW A-3
MOUNTAIN HOME . . . A-6
MOYIE SPRINGS . . . A-1
NAMPA A-6
NEW MEADOWS . . . A-4
PARIS D-7
PARMA A-5
PAYETTE A-5
PLUMMER A-2
POCATELLO D-7
POTLATCH A-3
PRESTON D-7
PRIEST RIVER A-1
REXBURG D-5
RICHFIELD C-6
RIGBY D-6
RIGGINS A-4
ROGERSON B-7
RUPERT C-7
SALMON C-4
SANDPOINT A-1
SHOSHONE C-6
SMITHS FERRY A-5
SODA SPRINGS D-6
SPENCER D-5
ST. ANTHONY D-5
STANLEY B-5
SUNBEAM B-5
TWIN FALLS B-7
WALLACE A-2
WEISER A-5
WHITE BIRD A-4
WINCHESTER A-3

MORRIS C-2
MORTON C-2
MOUNT CARMEL . . . D-6
MOUNT CARROLL . . B-1
MOUNT VERNON . . . C-6
MURPHYSBORO C-6
NASHVILLE C-6
NEW CASTLE D-4
OLNEY D-5
OREGON C-1
PANA C-5
PARIS D-4
PAXTON D-3
PEKIN B-3
PEORIA B-3
PEORIA HEIGHTS . . . C-3
PRINCETON B-2
QUINCY A-4
RANTOUL D-3
RED BUD B-6
ROCK FALLS C-2
ROCK ISLAND A-2
ROCKFORD C-1
ROSSVILLE D-3
RUSHVILLE B-4
SALEM C-5
SHAWNEETOWN . . . D-6
SPRINGFIELD B-4
STERLING B-2
STOCKTON B-1
SYCAMORE C-1
URBANA D-4
VANDALIA C-5
VIENNA C-7
WATERLOO B-6
WATSEKA D-3
WAUKEGAN D-1

MISHAWAKA C-1
MONTICELLO B-2
MOORESVILLE C-4
MOUNT VERNON . . . A-7
MUNCIE D-3
NASHVILLE C-5
NEW ALBANY C-6
NEW CASTLE D-4
NOBLESVILLE C-3
NORTH VERNON . . . D-5
PALMYRA C-6
PAOLI C-6
PERU C-2
PLYMOUTH C-2
PORTLAND D-3
PRINCETON A-6
RENSSELAER B-2
RICHMOND D-4
ROCKVILLE B-4
RUSHVILLE D-4
SEYMOUR C-5
SOUTH BEND B-1
SPENCER B-5
SULLIVAN B-5
TERRE HAUTE B-4
VALPARAISO B-1
VEEDERSBURG B-3
VERSAILLES D-5
WABASH C-2
WALKERTON C-1
WARSAW C-2
WASHINGTON B-6
WINAMAC B-2
WINCHESTER D-3
WORTHINGTON B-5

KANSAS

ABILENE E-2
ARKANSAS CITY . . . E-4
ARMA G-4
ATWOOD B-1
AUGUSTA E-4
BAXTER SPRINGS . . G-4
BELLEVILLE E-1
BLUE RAPIDS E-1
BUCKLIN C-4
BURLINGTON F-3
CALDWELL D-4
CANEY F-4
CHANUTE G-4
CHERRYVALE G-4
CIMARRON B-3
COFFEYVILLE G-4
CONCORDIA D-1
DERBY E-4
DODGE CITY B-3
DOUGLASS E-4
EL DORADO E-3
ELKHART A-4
ELLINWOOD C-3
ELLIS C-2
ELLSWORTH D-2
EMPORIA F-3
EUREKA F-3
FLORENCE E-3
FORT SCOTT G-3
GARNETT G-3
GOODLAND A-2
GREAT BEND C-3
GREENSBURG C-4
HAYS C-2
HAYSVILLE E-4
HERINGTON E-2
HILL CITY C-2
HOISINGTON C-3
HOLTON F-1
HUTCHINSON D-3
INDEPENDENCE F-4
IOLA G-3
JETMORE C-3
JUNCTION CITY E-2
KANSAS CITY G-2
KINGMAN D-4
KINSLEY C-3
LAKIN A-3
LARNED C-3
LAWRENCE F-2
LIBERAL B-4
LOUISBURG G-2
LYONS D-3
MANKATO D-1
MARYSVILLE F-1
MCPHERSON D-3
MEADE B-4

OGDEN C-3
OSAGE E-1
OSCEOLA D-4
OSKALOOSA D-3
OTTUMWA E-4
PARKERSBURG E-2
PERRY C-3
POSTVILLE F-1
RED OAK B-4
ROCK RAPIDS B-1
ROCKWELL CITY . . . C-2
SAC CITY C-2
SHELDON B-1
SHENANDOAH B-4
SIBLEY B-1
SIDNEY B-4
SIOUX CITY A-2
SPENCER B-1
SPIRIT LAKE B-1
STORM LAKE B-2
TAMA E-3
TRAER E-2
VINTON E-2
WAPELLO F-4
WATERLOO E-2
WAVERLY E-2
WEST UNION F-1
WILLIAMSBURG E-3
WINTERSET C-3
WOODBINE B-3

MEDICINE LODGE . . . D-4
MINNEOLA C-4
MORAN G-3
NEODESHA F-4
NESS CITY B-3
NEWTON D-3
NORTON C-1
OAKLEY B-2
OBERLIN B-1
OLATHE G-2
OSAWATOMIE G-3
OSBORNE C-2
OTTAWA G-2
PEABODY E-3
PHILLIPSBURG C-1
PITTSBURG G-4
PLEASANTON G-3
PRATT C-4
QUINTER B-2
RILEY E-2
RUSSELL C-2
SABETHA F-1
SALINA E-2
SCOTT CITY B-3
SENECA F-1
SHARON SPRINGS . . A-2
SMITH CENTER D-1
ST. FRANCIS A-1
ST. JOHN D-3
STAFFORD C-3
SYRACUSE A-3
TOPEKA F-2
TROY G-1
VICTORIA C-2
WAKEENEY C-2
WASHINGTON E-1
WICHITA E-4
WILSON D-2
WINFIELD E-4
YATES CENTER F-3

KENTUCKY

ALBANY E-4
ASHLAND F-2
BARDSTOWN D-3
BARDWELL A-4
BEDFORD D-2
BOWLING GREEN . . . C-3
BUTLER E-1
CAMPTON F-3
CENTRAL CITY C-3
CORBIN F-3
COVINGTON E-1
CUMBERLAND F-3
CYNTHIANA E-2
ELIZABETHTOWN . . . D-3
FRANKFORT D-2
FULTON A-4
GEORGETOWN E-2
GLASGOW D-3
GRAYSON F-2
GREENUP G-2
HARLAN F-3
HARRODSBURG E-3
HAZARD F-3
HENDERSON B-2
HODGENVILLE D-3
HOPKINSVILLE C-4
INEZ G-3
IRVINGTON D-2
JACKSON F-3
JAMESTOWN E-3
JENKINS G-3
LEITCHFIELD C-3
LEXINGTON E-2
LIVERMORE C-3
LONDON E-3
LOUISA G-2
LOUISVILLE D-2
MANCHESTER F-3
MARION B-3
MAYFIELD B-4
MAYSVILLE F-2
MIDDLESBORO E-4
MOREHEAD F-2
MORGANFIELD B-3
MT. VERNON E-3
MURRAY B-4
NEW CASTLE E-2

LOUISIANA

ALEXANDRIA C-2
BASTROP D-1
BATON ROUGE E-3
BERNICE C-1
BOSSIER CITY B-1
CAMPTI C-2
CLAYTON D-2
COLFAX C-2
COUSHATTA C-2
COVINGTON F-3
CROWLEY C-4
DE QUINCY B-3
DE RIDDER C-3
DELHI D-1
EUNICE C-3
FERRIDAY D-2
FRANKLIN D-4
GLENMORA C-3
GRAMBLING C-1
HAMMOND E-3
HOMER C-1
HOUMA E-4
JEANERETTE D-4
JENA D-2
JENNINGS C-4
JONESBORO C-1
JONESVILLE D-2
KENNER E-4
KENTWOOD E-3
KINDER C-3
LAFAYETTE D-4
LAKE CHARLES C-4
LAKE PROVIDENCE . D-1
LECOMPTE C-3
LEESVILLE B-3
LOGANSPORT B-2
MANSFIELD B-2
MANY C-2
MERRYVILLE B-3
METAIRIE E-4
MINDEN C-1
MONROE D-1
MONTGOMERY C-2
MORGAN CITY E-4
NEW IBERIA D-4
NEW ORLEANS F-4
OAKDALE C-3
OBERLIN C-3
OPELOUSAS D-3
PINEVILLE D-2
PLAQUEMINE D-3
PORT ALLEN D-3
PORT SULPHUR F-4
RAYNE D-4
RUSTON C-1
SHREVEPORT B-1
SLIDELL F-4
ST. FRANCISVILLE . . D-3
TALLULAH D-1
THIBODAUX E-4
TULLOS D-2
VENICE F-4
VIDALIA D-2
VINTON B-4
WELSH C-4
WINNFIELD C-2
WINNSBORO D-1
ZWOLLE B-2

OWENSBORO C-3
OWENTON E-2
PADUCAH B-3
PARIS E-2
PIKEVILLE G-3
PRESTONSBURG . . . G-3
PRINCETON B-3
RICHMOND E-3
RUSSELLVILLE C-4
SCOTTSVILLE D-4
SEBREE C-3
SOMERSET E-3
STANFORD E-3
VERSAILLES E-2
WHITESBURG F-3
WICKLIFFE A-3
WILLIAMSBURG E-4
WINCHESTER E-2

MAINE

ALFRED A-7
AMHERST D-5
AUBURN A-6
AUGUSTA B-5
BANGOR C-5
BAR HARBOR D-5
BATH B-6
BELFAST C-5
BETHEL A-5
BINGHAM B-4
BRUNSWICK B-6
BUCKSPORT C-5
CAMDEN C-6
CARIBOU D-2
CHERRYFIELD D-5
DANFORTH D-3
ELLSWORTH D-5
FARMINGTON A-5
FRYEBURG A-6
GRAY A-6
GUILFORD B-4
HARMONY B-4
HOLLIS CENTER A-6
HOULTON D-3
ISLE AU HAUT C-6
JACKMAN A-4
JONESBORO D-5
KITTERY A-7
LAGRANGE C-4
LEWISTON B-6
LINCOLN C-4
MACHIAS D-5
MARS HILL D-2
MILO C-4
MONTICELLO D-2
NEWRY A-5
NORWAY A-6
PERRY E-4
PORTLAND B-6
PRESQUE ISLE C-2
ROCKLAND B-6
RUMFORD A-5
SANFORD A-7
SKOWHEGAN B-5
SPRINGFIELD D-4
STONINGTON C-6
THOMASTON B-6
TOPSFIELD D-4
VAN BUREN D-1
WATERVILLE B-5
WESLEY D-4
WEST FORKS B-4
WHITING E-5
WINTHROP B-5
WISCASSET B-6
WOODLAND D-4
YARMOUTH B-6

MARYLAND

ABERDEEN F-1
ACCIDENT A-1
ANNAPOLIS E-2
BALTIMORE E-2
BEL AIR E-1
BERLIN G-4
BRANDYWINE E-3
CAMBRIDGE E-3
CLEAR SPRING C-1
COLUMBIA D-2
CRISFIELD F-4
CUMBERLAND B-1
DARLINGTON E-1
DENTON F-3
DUNDALK E-2
EASTON F-3
EDGEWOOD E-2
ELKTON F-1
EWELL F-4
FREDERICK D-1
FROSTBURG A-1
GERMANTOWN D-2
HAGERSTOWN C-1
HEREFORD E-1
INDIAN HEAD D-3
LA PLATA D-3
LEXINGTON PARK . . . E-4
OCEAN CITY G-4
POCOMOKE CITY . . . F-4
POPES CREEK D-3
POTOMAC D-2
PRINCE FREDERICK . E-3
QUEENSTOWN E-2
RANDALLSTOWN D-2

SALISBURY F-4
SCOTLAND E-4
SEVERNA PARK . . . E-2
SILVER SPRING D-2
SNOW HILL G-4
ST. CHARLES E-3
TIMONIUM E-1
UPPER MARLBORO . E-3
VIENNA F-3
WASHINGTON, DC . . E-3
WESTMINSTER D-1

MASSACHUSETTS

AMHERST C-2
BALDWINVILLE D-1
BEDFORD E-2
BELCHERTOWN C-2
BEVERLY E-2
BILLERICA E-2
BOSTON E-2
BOURNE F-4
BROCKTON E-3
BROOKFIELD C-2
CHARLEMONT B-1
CHATHAM G-4
CHELMSFORD E-2
CHICOPEE C-3
CHILMARK F-5
CUMMINGTON B-2
DALTON B-2
DANVERS F-2
EAST FREETOWN F-4
EDGARTOWN F-4
ERVING C-1
FALL RIVER F-4
FALMOUTH F-4
FITCHBURG D-2
FRAMINGHAM E-2
GAY HEAD F-5
GLOUCESTER F-1
GOSHEN B-2
GREAT
  BARRINGTON A-2
GREENFIELD B-2
HAVERHILL E-1
HOLYOKE C-2
HYANNIS G-4
LAWRENCE E-1
LEE A-2
LEOMINSTER D-2
LEXINGTON E-2
LOWELL E-1
LUDLOW C-3
LYNN E-2
MADAKET G-5
MALDEN E-2
MIDDLEBORO F-3
MILTON E-2
NANTUCKET G-5
NEW BEDFORD F-4
NEWBURYPORT F-1
NORTH ADAMS B-1
NORTH TISBURY F-4
NORTHAMPTON B-2
OAK BLUFFS F-4
PITTSFIELD A-2
PLYMOUTH F-3
PROVINCETOWN G-3
QUINCY E-2
RANDOLPH E-3
SALEM F-2
SALISBURY F-1
SHEFFIELD A-3
SOMERVILLE E-2
SPENCER D-2
SPRINGFIELD C-3
STURBRIDGE D-3
TAUNTON E-3
TRURO G-3
WARE C-2
WELLFLEET G-3
WESTFIELD B-3
WESTMINISTER C-2
WEYMOUTH F-2
WINCHENDON C-1
WINDSOR B-2
WORCESTER D-2

MICHIGAN

ALANSON A-3
ALBION D-6
ALLEGAN D-6
ALMA E-5

ALPENA E-3
ANN ARBOR E-6
ATLANTA E-3
AU GRES E-4
BAD AXE F-4
BALDWIN D-4
BARAGA B-1
BATTLE CREEK D-6
BAY CITY E-4
BENTON HARBOR . . C-6
BLANEY PARK D-2
BREVORT D-2
BRUCE CROSSING . . B-1
BURTON E-5
CADILLAC D-4
CEDAR SPRINGS . . . D-5
CHAMPION B-2
CHARLEVOIX D-3
CHARLOTTE D-5
CHEBOYGAN D-3
CLARE D-4
COPPER HARBOR . . . B-1
COVINGTON B-1
CRYSTAL FALLS B-2
DEARBORN E-6
DETROIT F-6
DOUGLAS C-5
DUNDEE E-6
DURAND E-5
EASTPORT D-3
ELK RAPIDS D-3
ELMIRA D-3
ESCANABA C-2
FENTON E-5
FLINT E-5
GAYLORD E-3
GLADSTONE C-2
GRAND HAVEN C-5
GRAND RAPIDS D-5
HANCOCK B-1
HARBOR BEACH F-4
HARRISVILLE F-3
HASTINGS D-5
HILLMAN E-3
HOLLAND C-5
HOUGHTON B-1
HOUGHTON LAKE . . . E-4
HOWARD CITY D-5
HURON BEACH E-3
IMLAY CITY F-5
IONIA D-5
IRON MOUNTAIN B-2
IRON RIVER B-2
IRONWOOD A-2
ISHPEMING B-2
JACKSON E-6
KALAMAZOO D-6
KALKASKA D-3
L'ANSE B-1
LANSING E-5
LEXINGTON F-5
LUDINGTON D-4
MACKINAW CITY E-2
MANCELONA D-3
MANISTEE D-4
MANISTIQUE C-2
MANTON D-4
MARLETTE F-5
MARQUETTE C-1
MARSHALL D-6
MASS CITY B-1
MENOMINEE E-3
MERRIWEATHER A-1
MUNISING C-2
MUSKEGON C-5
NEW BUFFALO C-6
NILES C-6
ONTONAGON A-1
OSCODA E-4
OWOSSO E-3
PETOSKEY D-3
PONTIAC E-5
PORT AUSTIN F-4
PORT HOPE F-4
PORT HURON F-5
PORT SANILAC F-4
PORTLAND D-5
POWERS B-2
RAPID RIVER C-2
REED CITY D-4
ROMEO E-5
SAGINAW E-5
SAULT STE. MARIE . . E-2
SCOTTVILLE D-4
SEBEWAING E-4
SHEPHERD D-4
SHINGLETON C-2

SOUTH HAVEN C-6
ST. IGNACE E-2
ST. JOHNS E-5
ST. JOSEPH C-6
STANDISH E-4
STURGIS D-6
TAWAS CITY E-4
THREE RIVERS D-6
TRAVERSE CITY D-3
TRENARY C-2
WAKEFIELD A-2
WATERSMEET A-2
WAYLAND D-5
WEST BRANCH E-4
YPSILANTI E-6

MINNESOTA

AITKIN C-3
ALBERT LEA C-6
ALEXANDRIA B-4
AUSTIN C-6
BAUDETTE B-1
BEMIDJI B-3
BENSON B-4
BIG FALLS B-2
BLACKDUCK B-2
BLOOMINGTON C-5
BLUE EARTH C-6
BRAINERD C-4
BRECKENRIDGE A-4
CAMBRIDGE C-4
CANBY A-5
CANNON FALLS C-5
CARLTON C-3
CENTER CITY C-4
CHASKA C-5
CHISHOLM C-2
CLOQUET C-3
COOK C-2
CROOKSTON A-2
CROSBY C-4
DETROIT LAKES B-3
DULUTH D-3
EAST GRAND FORKS A-2
ELBOW LAKE A-4
ELK RIVER C-4
FAIRMONT B-6
FERGUS FALLS A-4
FLOODWOOD C-3
FOSSTON B-2
GLENCOE C-5
GRAND MARAIS E-2
GRAND PORTAGE . . . E-2
GRAND RAPIDS C-3
GRANITE FALLS A-5
GREENBUSH A-1
HALLOCK A-1
HAWLEY A-3
HIBBING C-3
HINCKLEY C-4
INTERNATIONAL
  FALLS C-1
JACKSON B-6
KARLSTAD A-2
LA CRESCENT D-6
LAKE BENTON A-5
LAKE CITY D-5
LITTLE FALLS C-4
LUVERNE A-6
MADELIA B-6
MAHNOMEN A-3
MANKATO C-6
MARSHALL B-5
MILACA C-4
MINNEAPOLIS C-5
MONTEVIDEO A-5
MOORHEAD A-3
MOOSE LAKE C-3
MORA C-4
NEW ULM B-5
OLIVIA B-5
ONAMIA C-4
ORTONVILLE A-4
OWATONNA C-5
PARK RAPIDS B-3
PINE CITY C-4
PINE RIVER C-3
PIPESTONE A-6
PRESTON D-6
PRINCETON C-4
RED WING D-5
REDWOOD FALLS . . . B-5
ROCHESTER D-6
ROSEAU B-1
SANDSTONE C-4
SAUK CENTRE B-4

SLEEPY EYE B-5
SPICER B-5
SPRING VALLEY D-6
SPRINGFIELD B-5
ST. CLOUD B-4
ST. JAMES B-6
ST. PAUL C-5
ST. PETER C-5
THIEF RIVER FALLS . . A-2
TRACY B-5
TWO HARBORS D-3
VIRGINIA D-2
WADENA B-3
WALKER B-3
WARREN A-2
WARROAD B-1
WASECA C-6
WILLMAR B-5
WORTHINGTON A-6

MISSISSIPPI

ABERDEEN D-2
AMORY D-2
BALDWYN D-1
BATESVILLE C-1
BAY SAINT LOUIS . . . C-7
BEAUMONT D-6
BELZONI B-3
BILOXI D-7
BOONEVILLE D-1
BROOKHAVEN B-5
CANTON C-4
CLARKSDALE B-2
CLEVELAND B-3
CLINTON B-5
COLLINS C-6
COLUMBIA C-6
COLUMBUS D-3
CORINTH D-1
CRYSTAL SPRINGS . . B-5
ELLISVILLE C-5
EUPORA C-3
FAYETTE A-5
FLORA B-4
GREENVILLE A-3
GREENWOOD C-3
GRENADA C-2
GULFPORT D-7
HATTIESBURG D-6
HAZLEHURST B-5
HERNANDO C-1
HOLLANDALE A-3
HOLLY SPRINGS C-1
HORN LAKE C-1
INDIANOLA B-3
JACKSON C-4
LAUDERDALE D-4
LAUREL C-6
LELAND B-3
LOUISVILLE C-3
LUCEDALE D-6
LUMBERTON C-6
MACON D-3
MADISON C-4
MAGNOLIA B-6
MARKS B-2
MATHISTON D-3
MCCOMB B-6
MEADVILLE B-5
MENDENHALL C-5
MERIDIAN D-4
MONTICELLO B-6
MOUNT OLIVE C-5
NATCHEZ A-6
NEW ALBANY D-1
NEWTON D-4
OAKLAND C-2
OKOLONA D-2
OXFORD C-1
PASCAGOULA D-7
PICAYUNE C-7
PONTOTOC D-2
POPLARVILLE C-6
PORT GIBSON B-5
PRENTISS C-5
PURVIS C-6
QUITMAN D-4
REDWOOD B-4
ROLLING FORK B-4
RULEVILLE B-3
SENATOBIA C-1
STARKVILLE D-3
STATE LINE D-6
TCHULA B-3
TUNICA B-1
TUPELO D-2

TUTWILER B-2
TYLERTOWN C-6
VAIDEN C-3
VICKSBURG B-5
WALNUT D-1
WAYNESBORO D-5
WEST POINT D-3
WIGGINS D-7
WINONA C-3
WOODVILLE A-6
YAZOO CITY B-4

MISSOURI

ALBANY B-1
ALTON D-5
ANDERSON B-5
BETHANY B-1
BOLIVAR C-4
BOONVILLE C-2
BOWLING GREEN . . . D-2
BRANSON C-5
BUFFALO C-4
CABOOL D-4
CAMDENTON C-4
CAMPBELL F-5
CAPE GIRARDEAU . . E-4
CARROLLTON B-2
CARTHAGE B-4
CHILLICOTHE C-2
CLINTON B-3
COLUMBIA C-2
CONCORDIA B-3
CUBA D-3
DEXTER F-5
DONIPHAN E-5
EL DORADO
  SPRINGS B-4
ELDON C-3
FARMINGTON E-4
FESTUS E-3
FREDERICKTOWN . . . E-4
FULTON D-3
GRANT CITY B-1
GREENFIELD B-4
HAMILTON B-2
HANNIBAL D-2
HARRISONVILLE B-3
HOUSTON D-4
INDEPENDENCE B-2
JACKSON F-4
JEFFERSON CITY . . . D-3
JOPLIN B-5
KAHOKA D-1
KANSAS CITY B-2
KENNETT F-5
KING CITY B-1
KIRKSVILLE C-1
LAMAR B-4
LINN D-3
MACON C-2
MALDEN E-5
MANSFIELD C-5
MARSHALL C-2
MARYVILLE B-1
MEMPHIS D-1
MEXICO D-2
MOBERLY D-2
MONETT B-5
MONROE CITY D-2
NEOSHO B-5
NEVADA B-4
NEW LONDON D-2
NEW MADRID F-5
OSCEOLA B-4
OZARK C-5
PARIS D-2
PERRYVILLE E-4
POPLAR BLUFF E-5
POTOSI E-4
PRINCETON C-1
RICH HILL B-3
ROCK PORT A-1
ROLLA D-4
SEDALIA C-3
SIKESTON F-5
SPRINGFIELD C-4
ST. CHARLES E-3
ST. CLAIR E-3
ST. JAMES D-3
ST. JOSEPH B-2
ST. LOUIS E-3
STANBERRY B-1
SWEET SPRINGS . . . C-3
THAYER D-5
TIPTON C-3
TRENTON C-1

MONTANA

ALZADA G-4
ANACONDA B-3
ASHLAND F-4
BAKER G-3
BARBER D-3
BELT C-2
BIG SANDY D-1
BIG TIMBER D-3
BILLINGS E-3
BOULDER C-3
BOZEMAN C-4
BRIDGER E-4
BROADUS G-4
BROADVIEW D-3
BROWNING B-1
BUTTE C-3
CASCADE C-2
CHESTER C-1
CHINOOK D-1
CHOTEAU C-2
CIRCLE F-2
COLUMBUS D-4
CONRAD C-1
CRAIG C-2
CULBERTSON G-1
CUT BANK C-1
DARBY B-3
DEER LODGE B-3
DELL B-4
DILLON B-4
DIVIDE B-3
DODSON E-1
DUTTON C-2
EAST HELENA C-3
EDGAR E-4
EUREKA A-1
EVERGREEN B-1
FALLON G-3
FORSYTH F-3
FORT BENTON D-2
FORTINE A-1
FRAZER F-2
FROMBERG E-4
GARRYOWEN F-3
GLASGOW F-1
GLEN B-4
GLENDIVE G-2
GREAT FALLS C-2
HAMILTON B-3
HAMMOND G-4
HARDIN E-3
HARLEM D-1
HARLOWTON D-3
HAVRE D-1
HELENA B-3
HINGHAM D-1
HINSDALE F-1
HOBSON D-2
HYSHAM E-3
JORDAN F-2
JUDITH GAP D-3
KALISPELL A-1
KINSEY F-3
KIOWA B-1
LAME DEER F-3
LAREDO D-1
LAUREL D-3
LEWISTOWN D-2
LIMA B-4
LINCOLN B-2
LINDSAY G-2
LIVINGSTON D-4
LODGE GRASS F-4
LOMA D-2
MALTA E-1
MANHATTAN C-4
MILES CITY F-3
MINER D-4
MISSOULA B-2
MOSBY E-2
NASHUA F-1
OLNEY A-1
PLEVNA G-3
POLSON A-2

POPLAR G-1
RED LODGE D-4
ROUNDUP E-3
SACO E-1
SHELBY C-1
ST. IGNATIUS A-2
STANFORD D-2
SULA B-3
SUNBURST C-1
TERRY F-3
TOWNSEND C-3
TROY A-1
WEST
  YELLOWSTONE . . . C-4
WHITEFISH A-1
WIBAUX G-2
WINNETT E-2
WOLF POINT F-2
ZURICH D-1

NEBRASKA

AINSWORTH D-2
ALLIANCE B-2
ALMA D-4
ANSELMO D-3
ANSLEY D-3
ARAPAHOE D-4
ATKINSON D-2
AUBURN G-4
BARTLETT E-2
BASSETT D-2
BATTLE CREEK F-2
BAYARD A-2
BEATRICE F-4
BELLEVUE G-3
BLAIR G-3
BLUE HILL E-4
BRIDGEPORT A-2
BROKEN BOW D-3
CAMBRIDGE C-4
CERESCO F-3
CHADRON A-1
CODY C-1
COLUMBUS F-3
CRAWFORD A-1
CRETE F-3
CROFTON F-1
CULBERTSON C-4
DALTON B-2
DALTON A-3
DONIPHAN E-3
DUNNING D-2
ELWOOD D-4
FAIRBURY F-4
FAIRMONT F-4
FRANKLIN F-3
FREMONT F-3
FRIEND F-4
GENEVA F-4
GORDON B-1
GRAND ISLAND E-3
GREELEY E-3
HAIGLER C-4
HARRISON A-1
HASTINGS E-4
HAY SPRINGS B-1
HEBRON F-4
HOLDREGE D-4
HUMPHREY F-2
HYANNIS B-2
IMPERIAL C-4
KIMBALL A-3
LEWELLEN B-3
LINCOLN F-3
LONG PINE D-2
LYONS F-2
MADISON E-2
MAYWOOD C-4
MCCOOK C-4
MERRIMAN B-1
MINDEN E-4
MITCHELL A-2
MORRILL A-2
MULLEN C-2
NEBRASKA CITY G-3
NELIGH E-2
NORFOLK F-2
NORTH BEND F-3
NORTH PLATTE C-3
OGALLALA B-3
OMAHA G-3
O'NEILL E-2
OSCEOLA F-3
OSHKOSH B-3
PALISADE C-4
PAPILLION G-3

INDEX

PLAINVIEW E-2
PLATTSMOUTH G-3
RANDOLPH F-2
RAVENNA D-3
RED CLOUD E-4
RUSHVILLE B-1
S. SIOUX CITY F-2
SARGENT D-2
SCHUYLER F-3
SCOTTSBLUFF A-2
SIDNEY A-3
SPENCER E-1
SPRINGVIEW D-1
ST. PAUL E-3
STAPLETON C-3
STROMSBURG F-3
STUART D-1
SUTTON E-4
TAYLOR D-2
TECUMSEH F-4
THEDFORD C-2
TRENTON C-4
VALENTINE C-1
WAHOO F-3
WAUNETA C-4
WELLFLEET C-3
WINNEBAGO F-2
WISNER F-2
WOOD LAKE D-1
WYMORE F-4
YORK F-3

NEVADA
AMARGOSA VALLEY C-6
ASH SPRINGS D-5
AUSTIN C-3
BASALT B-4
BATTLE MOUNTAIN B-2
BEATTY C-6
CALIENTE D-5
CARLIN C-2
CARSON CITY A-4
COALDALE B-5
CURRANT D-4
CURRIE D-3
ELKO D-2
ELY D-3
EUREKA C-3
FALLON B-3
FERNLEY A-3
GLENDALE D-6
GOLCONDA B-2
GOLDFIELD C-5
HALLECK D-2
HAWTHORNE A-4
HENDERSON D-6
JACKPOT D-1
LAGES D-3
LAS VEGAS C-6
LAUGHLIN D-7
LOVELOCK A-3
LUNING B-4
MCDERMITT B-1
MESQUITE D-6
MIDDLEGATE B-3
MILL CITY B-2
NORTH LAS VEGAS D-6
OREANA B-2
OROVADA B-1
PANACA D-5
PIOCHE D-5
RENO A-3
SCHURZ A-4
SCOTTY'S JUNCTION C-5
SILVER SPRINGS A-3
SPARKS A-3
TONOPAH C-5
TOPAZ LAKE A-4
WARM SPRINGS D-5
WELLS D-2
WEST WENDOVER D-2
WILKINS D-1
WINNEMUCCA B-2

NEW HAMPSHIRE
ALTON C-5
ANTRIM B-6
COLEBROOK B-6
CONCORD B-6
CONWAY C-4
ERROL C-2
GLEN C-4
GORHAM C-3
HILLSBORO B-6
JAFFREY B-7
KEENE A-7
LANCASTER C-3
LITTLETON B-3
MANCHESTER C-5
MEREDITH B-5
NASHUA C-7
NORTH STRATFORD C-2
NORTHWOOD C-6
PORTSMOUTH D-6
ROCHESTER C-6
STEWARTSTOWN C-2
TROY A-7
TWIN MOUNTAIN C-3
UNION C-5
WEST OSSIPEE C-4
WOODSVILLE B-4

NEW JERSEY
ANDOVER B-2
ASBURY PARK D-4
ATLANTIC CITY C-6
BELMAR D-4
BERLIN B-5
BORDENTOWN C-4
BRIGANTINE C-6
BURLINGTON B-4
BUTLER C-2
CAMDEN B-4
CAPE MAY B-7
CHERRY HILL B-5
CHESTER B-2
DENNISVILLE B-7
EAST ORANGE D-2
EDISON C-3
ELIZABETH D-2
ELMER A-6
FAIRFIELD C-2
FRANKLIN C-1
FREEHOLD C-4
HACKENSACK D-2
HAINESVILLE B-1
HAMMONTON B-5
HEDGER HOUSE B-5
HIGHLANDS D-3
INDIAN MILLS B-5
JERSEY CITY D-2
LAKEWOOD C-4
LONG BRANCH D-4
MANALAPAN C-4
MANASQUAN D-4
MARLTON B-5
MAYS LANDING B-6
NETCONG C-2
NEW BRUNSWICK B-3
NEWARK C-2
NEWTON C-1
NORTH CAPE MAY B-7
OCEAN CITY C-6
PARAMUS D-2
PASSAIC D-2
PATERSON C-2
PERTH AMBOY C-3
PHILLIPSBURG B-2
PLAINFIELD C-3
POINT PLEASANT D-4
PRINCETON C-3
RAMSEY D-1
RED BANK D-3
SEASIDE HEIGHTS D-4
SHIP BOTTOM D-5
SILVERTON D-4
SOMERVILLE C-3
SOUTH RIVER C-3
SPARTA C-1
TOMS RIVER C-4
TRENTON B-4
UNION C-1
WOODSTOWN A-5

NEW MEXICO
ABBOTT D-2
ABIQUIU C-2
ALAMOGORDO C-5
ALBUQUERQUE B-3
ALMA A-4
ANTHONY B-6
ARTESIA D-5
AZTEC B-1
BELEN B-3
BERNALILLO B-2
BERNARDO B-3
BINGHAM C-4
BLOOMFIELD B-1
BUCKHORN A-5
CABALLO B-5
CAPITAN C-4
CAPROCK E-4
CARLSBAD D-5
CARRIZOZO C-4
CASA BLANCA B-3
CIMARRON D-1
CLAYTON E-1
CLINES CORNERS C-3
CLOVIS E-3
CORONA C-4
CUBA B-2
DATIL A-4
DEMING A-5
DILIA D-3
DURAN C-4
EAGLE NEST C-1
ELIDA E-4
ELK D-5
ELKINS E-4
ENCINO C-4
ESPANOLA C-2
FARMINGTON A-1
FORT SUMNER D-3
GALLUP A-2
GRANTS B-3
HATCH B-5
HOBBS E-5
HONDO C-4
HOPE D-5
HURLEY A-5
LAS CRUCES B-5
LAS VEGAS C-2
LOGAN E-3
LORDSBURG A-5
LOS LUNAS C-3
LOVINGTON E-5
MAGDALENA B-4
MALAGA E-5
MAXWELL D-1
MORIARTY C-3
MOUNTAINAIR C-3
NADINE E-5
NAGEEZI B-2
NARA VISA E-2
NASCHITTI A-2
NEWKIRK D-3
ORGAN B-5
OROGRANDE C-4
OSCURRO C-4
PIE TOWN A-3
POJOAQUE C-2
PORTALES E-4
QUEMADO A-3
RAMON D-4
RATON D-1
RIBERA C-2
RODEO A-6
ROSWELL D-4
SAN ACACIA B-3
SAN ANTONIO B-4
SAN JON E-3
SANTA FE C-2
SANTA ROSA D-3
SEPAR A-5
SEVEN RIVERS D-5
SHIPROCK A-1
SILVER CITY A-5
SOCORRO B-4
SPRINGER D-2
TAOS C-1
TATUM E-4
TIERRA AMARILLA B-1
TRUTH OR CONSEQUENCES B-4
TUCUMCARI D-3
TULAROSA C-5
VAUGHN C-4
WAGON MOUND D-2
WATROUS D-2
WHITES CITY D-5
WILLARD C-3
YESO D-3
ZUNI PUEBLO A-3

NEW YORK
ADAMS D-2
ALBANY E-3
ALDER CREEK D-3
ALEXANDRIA BAY D-1
AMENIA F-4
AMSTERDAM E-3
ANDES E-4
ANTWERP D-2
AUBURN C-3
BATH C-4
BEACON F-5
BINGHAMTON D-4
BUFFALO A-3
CAIRO E-4
CANTON D-1
CAPE VINCENT D-2
CATSKILL F-4
CAZENOVIA C-3
CHATEAUGAY E-1
CHEEKTOWAGA C-3
CORNING C-4
CORTLAND C-3
DANSVILLE B-4
DELHI E-4
DEPOSIT D-4
DRESDEN C-3
DRYDEN D-4
DUNKIRK A-4
EAST HAMPTON G-5
EAST ISLIP F-6
ELLICOTTVILLE A-4
ELMIRA C-4
ESPERANCE E-3
FINE E-1
FLEISCHMANNS E-4
FRANKLINVILLE B-4
FREDONIA A-4
FULTON C-3
GENESEO C-3
GENEVA C-3
GOUVERNEUR D-1
GOWANDA A-4
GREAT NECK F-5
GREECE B-3
GREENE D-4
GREENPORT G-5
HAMBURG A-3
HAMPTON BAYS G-5
HANCOCK D-4
HARRISVILLE D-2
HARTWICK D-3
HERKIMER E-3
HICKSVILLE F-6
HORNELL B-4
HUDSON FALLS F-3
HUNTINGTON STATION F-5
ILION D-3
INDIAN LAKE E-2
ITHACA C-4
JAMESTOWN A-4
KINGSTON F-4
LAKE CLEAR JUNCTION E-1
LAKE GEORGE E-2
LAKE PLACID F-1
LIBERTY E-4
LIMA B-3
LIMESTONE A-4
LOCKPORT B-3
LONG BEACH F-6
LONG LAKE E-2
LOWVILLE D-2
LYONS C-3
LYONS FALLS D-2
MALONE E-1
MASSENA E-1
MASTIC BEACH G-6
MATTITUCK G-5
MAYVILLE A-4
MECHANICVILLE F-3
MONTAUK G-5
MONTICELLO E-5
MORRISTOWN D-1
NASSAU F-3
NEW CITY E-5
NEW YORK F-6
NEWARK E-6
NEWBURGH E-5
NIAGARA FALLS A-3
NORWICH D-4
OGDENSBURG D-1
OLCOTT B-3
OLD FORGE E-2
OLEAN B-4
ONEONTA D-4
OSWEGO C-2
OWEGO D-4
PASSAIC E-5
PEEKSKILL F-5
PHOENICIA E-4
PLATTSBURGH F-1
PORT JEFFERSON F-5
POTSDAM E-1
POUGHKEEPSIE F-4
PRATTSVILLE E-4
PULASKI D-2
RIVERHEAD G-5
ROCHESTER C-3
ROCKY PT. F-5
ROME D-3
ROSCOE E-4
SACKETS HARBOR D-2
SALAMANCA A-4
SARATOGA SPRINGS E-3
SCHENECTADY F-3
SHERMAN A-4
SILVER CREEK A-3
SODUS C-3
SOMERVILLE E-6
SPECULATOR E-2
SYRACUSE C-3
TROY F-3
TUPPER LAKE E-2
UTICA D-3
WADDINGTON D-1
WARSAW B-3
WATERTOWN D-2
WATERVILLE D-3
WATKINS GLEN C-4
WELLSVILLE B-4
WESTFIELD A-4
WHITE PLAINS F-5
WHITEHALL F-2
YONKERS E-5

NORTH CAROLINA
ALBEMARLE D-2
ASHEBORO D-2
ASHEVILLE B-2
ATLANTIC G-3
BLACK MOUNTAIN B-2
BOONE B-2
BREVARD B-2
BRYSON CITY A-2
BURGAW E-3
BURLINGTON D-2
BUXTON G-2
CAROLINA BEACH F-4
CARTHAGE D-2
CARY E-2
CHARLOTTE C-2
CLINTON E-3
COLUMBIA G-2
CONCORD C-2
DUNN E-2
DURHAM E-2
EDENTON F-2
ELIZABETH CITY F-1
ELIZABETHTOWN E-3
FAYETTEVILLE D-3
FOREST CITY B-2
FRANKLIN A-2
GASTONIA C-2
GOLDSBORO E-2
GREENSBORO D-2
GREENVILLE F-2
HAMLET D-3
HATTERAS G-2
HAVELOCK F-3
HENDERSON E-1
HENDERSONVILLE B-2
HICKORY C-2
HIGH POINT D-2
JACKSONVILLE F-3
JEFFERSON C-1
KANNAPOLIS C-2
KINSTON F-2
KITTY HAWK G-1
LAURINBURG D-3
LENOIR C-2
LEXINGTON D-2
LOUISBURG E-2
LUMBERTON E-3
MADISON D-1
MAIDEN C-2
MANTEO G-1
MONROE C-3
MOREHEAD CITY F-3
MORGANTON C-2
MOUNT AIRY C-1
MOUNT OLIVE E-2
MURPHY A-2
NEW BERN F-2
NEWTON C-2
OCRACOKE G-3
OCRACOKE G-3
OXFORD E-1
PINEHURST D-2
PLYMOUTH F-2
RALEIGH E-2
REIDSVILLE D-1
RICHLANDS F-3
ROANOKE RAPIDS E-1
ROBBINSVILLE A-2
ROCKY MOUNT F-1
ROXBORO E-1
SALISBURY C-2
SALVO G-2
SANFORD D-2
SHALLOTTE E-4
SILER CITY D-2
SMITHFIELD E-2
SNOW HILL F-2
SUNSET BEACH E-4
SWANQUARTER G-2
SYLVA B-2
TABOR CITY E-3
TOPSAIL BEACH F-3
VANCEBORO F-2
WADESBORO D-3
WARSAW E-3
WASHINGTON F-2
WAYNESVILLE B-2
WHITEVILLE E-3
WILKESBORO C-2
WILLIAMSTON F-2
WILMINGTON E-3
WILSON E-2
WINDSOR F-2
WINSTON-SALEM C-1
WINTON F-1

NORTH DAKOTA
ALEXANDER A-2
AMIDON A-4
ANAMOOSE D-2
BALFOUR D-2
BEACH A-3
BELFIELD B-3
BERTHOLD C-2
BISMARCK D-3
BOTTINEAU D-1
BOWBELLS B-1
BOWMAN A-4
CANDO E-1
CARRINGTON E-3
CAVALIER F-1
CHURCHS FERRY E-2
COLEHARBOR C-2
COLFAX G-4
CROSBY B-1
DEVILS LAKE E-2
DICKINSON B-3
DRAKE D-2
DRAYTON F-1
DUNSEITH D-1
EDGELEY E-4
ELLENDALE E-4
FARGO G-3
FESSENDEN E-2
FORTUNA A-1
GARDNER G-3
GLADSTONE B-3
GRAND FORKS G-2
GRANVILLE D-2
GREAT BEND G-4
HAVANA F-4
HAZELTON D-4
HETTINGER B-4
HORACE G-3
JAMESTOWN E-3
KENMARE B-1
KNOX E-1
LAKOTA F-2
LANGDON E-1
LEEDS E-2
LINTON D-4
MANDAN C-3
MANVEL G-2
MARMARTH A-4
MEDINA E-3
MEDORA A-3
MINNEWAUKAN E-2
MINOT C-2
MOHALL C-1
MONANGO E-4
NECHE F-1
NEW ROCKFORD E-2
NEW SALEM C-3
NOONAN B-1
PEMBINA F-1
PETERSBURG F-2
RAY B-1
REYNOLDS G-2
RICHARDTON B-3
ROCKLAKE E-1
ROLLA E-1
ROSS B-2
SAWYER C-2
SCRANTON B-4
STANLEY B-2
STEELE D-3
STRASBURG D-4
TOLLEY D-1
TOWNER D-1
UNDERWOOD C-3
VALLEY CITY F-3
VELVA D-2
WAHPETON G-4
WASHBURN C-2
WATFORD CITY A-2
WILLISTON A-2
WILTON D-3

OHIO
AKRON D-2
ANTWERP A-2
ASHLAND C-2
ASHTABULA E-1
ATHENS D-5
BELLEVUE C-2
BETHEL A-5
BOWLING GREEN B-2
BRYAN A-1
BUCYRUS C-2
CADIZ E-3
CALDWELL E-4
CAMBRIDGE D-4
CANTON E-2
CHILLICOTHE C-5
CINCINNATI A-5
CIRCLEVILLE C-4
CLEVELAND D-1
CLYDE C-2
COLUMBUS C-4
CONNEAUT E-1
CORTLAND E-2
COSHOCTON D-3
DAYTON A-4
DEFIANCE A-2
DELAWARE C-3
DELPHOS A-2
DOVER E-3
EAST LIVERPOOL E-2
EATON A-4
ELYRIA D-2
EUCLID D-1
FINDLAY B-2
FOSTORIA C-2
FRANKLIN A-4
FREMONT C-2
GALION C-3
GALLIPOLIS C-6
GREENVILLE A-4
HAMILTON A-5
HILLSBORO B-5
JACKSON C-5
KENT E-2
KENTON B-3
LANCASTER C-4
LIMA A-3
LISBON E-2
LODI D-2
LOGAN C-4
LORAIN D-1
MANSFIELD D-5
MARIETTA D-5
MARION B-3
MARTINS FERRY F-3
MARYSVILLE B-3
MASSILLON D-2
MAUMEE B-1
MECHANICSBURG B-4
MEDINA D-2
MILFORD A-5
MILLERSBURG D-3
MINERVA E-3
MOUNT STERLING C-4
MOUNT VERNON C-3
NAPOLEON A-2
NEW PHILADELPHIA E-3
NEWARK C-4
NEWCOMERSTOWN D-3
NORWALK C-2
OTTAWA A-2
PAINESVILLE E-1
PEEBLES B-6
PIQUA A-3
POMEROY D-5
PORT CLINTON C-1
PORTSMOUTH B-6
RAVENNA E-2
RIPLEY B-6
SALEM E-2
SANDUSKY C-1
SIDNEY B-3
SOMERSET D-4
SOUTH POINT C-6
SPRINGFIELD B-4
ST. CLAIRSVILLE E-3
ST. MARYS A-3
STEUBENVILLE E-3
TOLEDO B-1
TROY B-4
UHRICHSVILLE E-3
UPPER SANDUSKY C-2
URBANA B-4
UTICA D-3
VAN WERT A-2
WAPAKONETA B-3
WARREN E-2
WASHINGTON COURT HOUSE B-5
WAVERLY C-5
WILLARD C-2
WILMINGTON B-5
WOODVILLE B-1
XENIA B-4
YOUNGSTOWN E-2
ZANESVILLE D-4

OKLAHOMA
ADA F-3
ALTUS D-3
ALVA D-1
ANADARKO D-3
ANTLERS G-4
APACHE D-3
ARDMORE E-4
ARNETT C-2
ATOKA F-4
BARTLESVILLE F-1
BLACKWELL E-1
BOISE CITY A-1
BOSWELL F-4
BRIDGEPORT D-2
BRISTOW F-2
BROKEN ARROW F-2
BROKEN BOW G-4
BUFFALO C-1
BURBANK F-1
CADDO F-3
CALVIN F-3
CHANDLER E-2
CHECOTAH G-3
CHEROKEE D-1
CHEYENNE C-2
CHICKASHA E-3
CLAREMORE F-2
CLAYTON G-3
CLEO SPRINGS D-1
CLINTON D-2
COALGATE F-3
COLBERT F-4
CORDELL D-3
CUSHING E-2
DAVIDSON D-3
DOVER E-2
DUKE C-3
DUNCAN E-3
DURANT F-4
EDMOND E-2
EL RENO E-2
ELGIN D-3
ELK CITY C-3
ENID D-2
EUFAULA F-3

FAIRVIEW . . . D-2
FORGAN . . . C-1
FORT SUPPLY . . . C-1
FREDERICK . . . D-4
GEARY . . . D-2
GUTHRIE . . . D-2
GUYMON . . . B-1
HARDESTY . . . B-1
HARTSHORNE . . . G-3
HEAVENER . . . G-3
HENRYETTA . . . F-2
HOLDENVILLE . . . F-3
HOLLIS . . . C-3
HUGO . . . G-4
IDABEL . . . G-4
JAY . . . G-2
KANSAS . . . G-2
KINGFISHER . . . E-2
KINGSTON . . . F-4
LAWTON . . . D-3
MANGUM . . . C-3
MARIETTA . . . E-3
MARLOW . . . E-3
MAY . . . C-1
MCALESTER . . . F-3
MEDFORD . . . E-1
MIAMI . . . G-1
MUSKOGEE . . . G-2
NASH . . . D-1
NORMAN . . . E-2
NOWATA . . . F-1
OKLAHOMA CITY . . . E-2
OKMULGEE . . . F-2
ORLANDO . . . E-2
PAULS VALLEY . . . E-3
PAWHUSKA . . . F-1
PAWNEE . . . F-1
PERRY . . . E-1
PONCA CITY . . . E-1
POND CREEK . . . E-1
POTEAU . . . G-3
PRYOR CREEK . . . G-2
PURCELL . . . E-3
RANDLETT . . . D-4
RATLIFF CITY . . . D-3
ROOSEVELT . . . D-3
ROSSTON . . . C-1
SALLISAW . . . G-2
SAPULPA . . . F-2
SAYRE . . . C-3
SEILING . . . D-2
SEMINOLE . . . E-3
SHAWNEE . . . E-3
SMITHVILLE . . . G-3
SNYDER . . . D-3
STILLWATER . . . E-2
STILWELL . . . G-2
STROUD . . . E-2
SULPHUR . . . E-3
TAHLEQUAH . . . G-2
TALOGA . . . D-2
TEXHOMA . . . A-1
TEXOLA . . . C-3
TULSA . . . F-2
VINITA . . . G-1
WATONGA . . . D-2
WAURIKA . . . E-4
WAYNOKA . . . D-1
WEATHERFORD . . . D-3
WESTVILLE . . . G-3
WETUMKA . . . F-3
WILBURTON . . . G-3
WOODWARD . . . C-2

OREGON

ALBANY . . . B-2
ARLINGTON . . . D-1
ASHLAND . . . B-5
ASTORIA . . . B-1
BAKER . . . F-2
BANDON . . . A-4
BEAVERTON . . . B-1
BEND . . . D-3
BLY . . . D-5
BOARDMAN . . . E-1
BROOKINGS . . . A-5
BURNS . . . E-3
BURNS JUNCTION . . . F-4
CANNON BEACH . . . B-1
CANYON CITY . . . E-3
CAVE JUNCTION . . . A-5
CHILOQUIN . . . C-5
COBURG . . . B-3
COOS BAY . . . B-4
COQUILLE . . . B-4
CORVALLIS . . . B-2
COTTAGE GROVE . . . B-3
DAYVILLE . . . E-3
DEPOE BAY . . . A-2
DETROIT . . . C-2
DUNES CITY . . . A-3
EUGENE . . . B-3
FLORENCE . . . A-3
GOLD BEACH . . . A-4
GRANTS PASS . . . B-4
GRASS VALLEY . . . D-2
GRESHAM . . . C-1
HARBOR . . . A-5
HILLSBORO . . . B-1
HOOD RIVER . . . C-1
HUNTINGTON . . . G-3
IDANHA . . . C-2
JORDAN VALLEY . . . F-4
KLAMATH FALLS . . . C-5
LA GRANDE . . . F-2
LA PINE . . . C-3
LAKEVIEW . . . D-5
LEBANON . . . C-2
LINCOLN BEACH . . . A-2
LINCOLN CITY . . . A-2
LONG CREEK . . . E-3
LOWELL . . . C-3
MADRAS . . . D-2
MAUPIN . . . D-2
MCDERMITT . . . F-5
MCMINNVILLE . . . B-2
MEDFORD . . . B-5
MILL CITY . . . C-2
MITCHELL . . . D-3
NEWBERG . . . B-2
NEWPORT . . . A-2
NORTH BEND . . . B-3
NORTH POWDER . . . F-2
NYSSA . . . G-3
OAKRIDGE . . . C-3
ONTARIO . . . G-3
PENDLETON . . . E-1
PILOT ROCK . . . E-2
PORT ORFORD . . . A-4
PORTLAND . . . C-1
PRAIRIE CITY . . . E-2
PRINEVILLE . . . D-3
RAINIER . . . C-1
REDMOND . . . D-3
REEDSPORT . . . A-3
RHODODENDRON . . . C-2
RILEY . . . E-3
ROCKAWAY BEACH . . . B-1
SALEM . . . B-1
SEASIDE . . . B-1
SENECA . . . E-3
SHANIKO . . . D-2
SISTERS . . . D-2
SPRINGFIELD . . . B-3
ST. HELENS . . . C-1
SWEET HOME . . . C-2
TALENT . . . B-5
THE DALLES . . . D-1
TILLAMOOK . . . B-1
UKIAH . . . E-2
UNITY . . . F-2
VALE . . . F-3
WALDPORT . . . B-2
WASCO . . . D-1
WESTON . . . F-1
WINSTON . . . B-4
YACHATS . . . A-3

PENNSYLVANIA

ALLENTOWN . . . F-3
ALTOONA . . . C-4
BARNSBORO . . . C-3
BEAVER . . . A-3
BEDFORD . . . C-4
BERWICK . . . E-3
BETHEL PARK . . . A-4
BETHLEHEM . . . G-3
BLAIRSVILLE . . . B-3
BLAKELY . . . F-2
BLOOMSBURG . . . E-3
BROOKVILLE . . . C-3
CALIFORNIA . . . A-4
CANONSBURG . . . A-4
CARLISLE . . . E-4
CHAMBERSBURG . . . D-4
CHESTER . . . F-4
CLARION . . . B-2
CLEARFIELD . . . C-3
CORRY . . . B-1
COUDERSPORT . . . D-2
DANVILLE . . . E-3
DILLSBURG . . . E-4
DOYLESTOWN . . . G-4
DRIFTWOOD . . . C-2
DUBOIS . . . C-3
DUSHORE . . . E-2
EASTON . . . G-3
EBENSBURG . . . B-4
EDINBORO . . . A-1
EMMAUS . . . F-4
EMPORIUM . . . C-2
ERIE . . . A-1
FRANKLIN . . . A-2
FREDERICKSBURG . . . F-4
GALETON . . . D-2
GETTYSBURG . . . D-5
GIRARD . . . A-1
GREENSBURG . . . B-4
GREENVILLE . . . A-2
HARRISBURG . . . D-4
HAWLEY . . . G-2
HERSHEY . . . E-4
HOLLIDAYSBURG . . . C-4
HONESDALE . . . G-2
HUNTINGDON . . . D-4
INDIANA . . . B-3
JOHNSTOWN . . . B-4
KANE . . . C-2
KITTANNING . . . B-3
LANCASTER . . . F-4
LANSDALE . . . G-4
LAPORTE . . . E-2
LEBANON . . . E-4
LEHIGHTON . . . F-3
LEVITTOWN . . . G-4
LEWISBURG . . . E-3
LEWISTOWN . . . D-3
LIVERPOOL . . . E-3
LOCK HAVEN . . . D-3
MAHAFFEY . . . C-3
MANSFIELD . . . E-2
MCCANDLESS . . . A-3
MEADVILLE . . . A-2
MILFORD . . . G-2
MILTON . . . E-3
MONROEVILLE . . . B-4
MOUNT JOY . . . E-4
MOUNT UNION . . . D-4
MT. POCONO . . . G-3
MUNCY . . . E-2
NANTICOKE . . . F-2
NAZARETH . . . F-3
NEW BETHLEHEM . . . B-3
NEW CASTLE . . . A-3
NORRISTOWN . . . F-4
OIL CITY . . . A-2
PHILADELPHIA . . . B-4
PHILIPSBURG . . . C-3
PITTSBURGH . . . A-4
PORT MATILDA . . . C-3
POTTSTOWN . . . F-4
POTTSVILLE . . . F-3
PUNXSUTAWNEY . . . B-3
QUAKERTOWN . . . G-4
READING . . . F-4
RENOVO . . . D-2
RIDGWAY . . . C-2
SAYRE . . . E-1
SCRANTON . . . F-2
SELINSGROVE . . . E-3
SHAMOKIN . . . E-3
SHARON . . . A-2
SHEFFIELD . . . B-2
SHENANDOAH . . . F-3
SMETHPORT . . . C-1
ST. MARYS . . . C-2
STATE COLLEGE . . . D-3
SUNBURY . . . E-3
TAMAQUA . . . F-3
TIONESTA . . . B-2
TOWANDA . . . E-2
TROY . . . E-2
TUNKHANNOCK . . . F-2
UNION CITY . . . A-1
UNIONTOWN . . . B-4
WARREN . . . B-1
WASHINGTON . . . A-4
WAYNESBURG . . . A-4
WELLSBORO . . . D-2
WILKES-BARRE . . . F-2
WILLIAMSPORT . . . E-2
WINDBER . . . C-4
WYALUSING . . . F-2
YORK . . . E-4

RHODE ISLAND

CHEPACHET . . . B-2
CRANSTON . . . C-2
EAST GREENWICH . . . C-3
MIDDLETOWN . . . D-4
NARRAGANSETT PIER . . . C-4
NEWPORT . . . D-4
PAWTUCKET . . . C-2
PORTSMOUTH . . . D-3
PROVIDENCE . . . C-2
WARWICK . . . C-3
WEST WARWICK . . . B-3
WESTERLY . . . B-4
WOONSOCKET . . . C-1

SOUTH CAROLINA

ABBEVILLE . . . B-2
AIKEN . . . C-3
ANDERSON . . . B-2
BARNWELL . . . D-3
BEAUFORT . . . D-5
BENNETTSVILLE . . . E-2
CAMDEN . . . D-2
CHARLESTON . . . E-4
CHERAW . . . E-2
CHESTER . . . C-2
COLUMBIA . . . D-2
CONWAY . . . F-3
DILLON . . . E-2
FAIRFAX . . . C-4
FLORENCE . . . E-2
FURMAN . . . D-4
GEORGETOWN . . . F-3
GREENVILLE . . . B-1
GREENWOOD . . . B-2
HAMPTON . . . D-4
HILTON HEAD ISLAND . . . D-5
ISLE OF PALMS . . . E-4
JAMESTOWN . . . E-3
KERSHAW . . . D-2
LADSON . . . E-4
LAKE CITY . . . E-3
LANCASTER . . . D-2
LAURENS . . . C-2
LORIS . . . F-2
MANNING . . . E-3
MARION . . . F-2
MCCORMICK . . . B-3
MYRTLE BEACH . . . F-3
NEWBERRY . . . C-2
NORTH . . . D-3
ORANGEBURG . . . D-3
PORT ROYAL . . . D-5
RED BANK . . . D-3
ROCK HILL . . . C-1
SALUDA . . . C-2
SEABROOK ISLAND . . . E-4
SENECA . . . A-2
SPARTANBURG . . . C-1
ST. GEORGE . . . D-4
ST. MATTHEWS . . . D-3
SUMTER . . . D-3
TAYLORS . . . B-1
UNION . . . C-2
WALTERBORO . . . D-4
WHITMIRE . . . C-2
WINNSBORO . . . C-2
YORK . . . D-1

SOUTH DAKOTA

ABERDEEN . . . F-1
ALEXANDRIA . . . F-4
ARLINGTON . . . F-3
ARMOUR . . . F-4
ASHTON . . . F-2
BATESLAND . . . B-4
BELLE FOURCHE . . . A-2
BERESFORD . . . G-4
BLUNT . . . D-2
BOWDLE . . . E-1
BRISTOL . . . F-1
BROOKINGS . . . G-3
BUFFALO . . . A-1
BURKE . . . E-4
CANTON . . . G-4
COLOME . . . E-4
COTTONWOOD . . . C-3
CUSTER . . . A-3
DEADWOOD . . . A-2
DOLAND . . . F-2
DUPREE . . . C-2
EDGEMONT . . . A-4
ELK POINT . . . G-5
FAITH . . . B-2
FAULKTON . . . E-2
FRUITDALE . . . A-2
GETTYSBURG . . . D-2
GROTON . . . F-1
HAYES . . . C-3
HENRY . . . F-2
HIGHMORE . . . D-2
HILL CITY . . . A-3
HOT SPRINGS . . . A-4
HURON . . . E-3
IPSWICH . . . E-1
KADOKA . . . C-3
LA PLANT . . . D-2
LEAD . . . A-3
LEBANON . . . D-2
LEMMON . . . B-1
LUDLOW . . . A-1
MADISON . . . G-3
MARTIN . . . C-4
MAURINE . . . B-2
MCINTOSH . . . C-1
MCLAUGHLIN . . . D-1
MIDLAND . . . D-3
MILBANK . . . G-2
MILLER . . . E-2
MISSION . . . D-4
MITCHELL . . . F-3
MOBRIDGE . . . D-1
MOUND CITY . . . D-1
MUD BUTTE . . . B-2
MURDO . . . D-3
NEW EFFINGTON . . . G-1
NEWELL . . . A-2
OGLALA . . . B-4
OLIVET . . . F-4
PARADE . . . C-2
PHILIP . . . C-3
PIERRE . . . D-3
PINE RIDGE . . . B-4
PLANKINTON . . . E-3
PRINGLE . . . A-3
RAPID CITY . . . A-3
REDFIELD . . . E-2
REDIG . . . A-1
SALEM . . . G-3
SELBY . . . D-1
SIOUX FALLS . . . G-4
SPEARFISH . . . A-2
STAMFORD . . . C-3
STICKNEY . . . F-4
STURGIS . . . A-3
TILFORD . . . A-3
TYNDALL . . . F-4
VERMILLION . . . G-5
VETAL . . . C-4
WAGNER . . . F-4
WALL . . . B-3
WARNER . . . F-1
WATERTOWN . . . G-2
WAUBAY . . . G-2
WESSINGTON . . . E-3
WESTPORT . . . E-1
WHITE RIVER . . . D-4
WINNER . . . D-4
YANKTON . . . G-4

TENNESSEE

ALCOA . . . E-3
ATWOOD . . . B-2
BOLIVAR . . . B-3
BRISTOL . . . G-2
BROWNSVILLE . . . A-3
CHATTANOOGA . . . D-3
CHURCH HILL . . . F-2
CLARKSVILLE . . . C-2
CLEVELAND . . . E-3
COLUMBIA . . . C-3
COOKEVILLE . . . D-2
COVINGTON . . . A-3
CROSSVILLE . . . E-2
DAYTON . . . E-3
DICKSON . . . C-2
DUCKTOWN . . . E-3
DUNLAP . . . D-3
DYERSBURG . . . A-2
ELIZABETHTON . . . G-2
ERIN . . . C-2
FAYETTEVILLE . . . C-3
FRANKLIN . . . C-2
GREENEVILLE . . . F-2
HARRIMAN . . . E-2
HENDERSONVILLE . . . D-2
HUMBOLDT . . . B-3
HUNTINGDON . . . B-2
JACKSON . . . B-3
JAMESTOWN . . . E-2
JOHNSON CITY . . . F-2
KINGSPORT . . . G-2
KNOXVILLE . . . F-2
LA FOLLETTE . . . F-1
LAWRENCEBURG . . . C-3
LEBANON . . . D-2
LINDEN . . . B-3
LIVINGSTON . . . E-2
LORETTO . . . C-3
MANCHESTER . . . D-3
MARTIN . . . B-2
MARYVILLE . . . E-3
MCKENZIE . . . B-2
MCMINNVILLE . . . D-3
MEMPHIS . . . A-3
MILAN . . . B-2
MILLINGTON . . . A-3
MONTEAGLE . . . D-3
MORRISTOWN . . . F-2
MURFREESBORO . . . C-2
NASHVILLE . . . C-2
NEW MARKET . . . F-2
OAK RIDGE . . . E-2
ONEIDA . . . E-2
PARIS . . . B-2
PULASKI . . . C-3
RIPLEY . . . A-3
ROCKWOOD . . . E-2
SAVANNAH . . . B-3
SELMER . . . B-3
SEVIERVILLE . . . F-3
SHARON . . . B-2
SOMERVILLE . . . A-3
SPRINGFIELD . . . C-2
TAZEWELL . . . F-1
TULLAHOMA . . . D-3
UNION CITY . . . A-2
WAVERLY . . . C-2
WAYNESBORO . . . B-3
WINCHESTER . . . D-3

TEXAS

ABILENE . . . D-3
ALBANY . . . D-3
ALICE . . . E-6
ALPINE . . . B-4
AMARILLO . . . C-1
ANDREWS . . . C-3
ANGLETON . . . G-5
ANSON . . . D-3
ARANSAS PASS . . . F-6
ARLINGTON . . . E-3
ATHENS . . . F-3
AUSTIN . . . E-4
BALLINGER . . . D-4
BALMORHEA . . . B-4
BAY CITY . . . F-5
BAYTOWN . . . G-5
BEAUMONT . . . G-5
BEEVILLE . . . E-6
BIG LAKE . . . C-4
BIG SPRING . . . C-4
BOGATA . . . G-3
BOWIE . . . E-3
BRACKETTVILLE . . . D-5
BRADY . . . D-4
BRECKENRIDGE . . . E-3
BRENHAM . . . F-5
BROWNFIELD . . . C-2
BROWNSVILLE . . . E-7
BROWNWOOD . . . D-4
BRYAN . . . F-4
BUFFALO . . . F-4
BURLESON . . . E-3
BURNET . . . E-4
CAMERON . . . F-4
CANADIAN . . . D-1
CANYON . . . C-2
CARRIZO SPRINGS . . . D-6
CARTHAGE . . . G-3
CEDAR PARK . . . E-4
CENTER . . . G-4
CHANNING . . . C-1
CHILDRESS . . . D-2
CHRISTOVAL . . . D-4
CISCO . . . E-3
CLARENDON . . . D-2
CLEVELAND . . . G-5
CLUTE . . . G-5
COLEMAN . . . D-4
COLORADO CITY . . . D-3
COMANCHE . . . E-4
COMSTOCK . . . C-5
CONROE . . . F-5
CORPUS CHRISTI . . . E-6
CORRIGAN . . . G-4
CORSICANA . . . F-4
COTULLA . . . D-6
CROCKETT . . . F-4
CRYSTAL CITY . . . D-6
CUERO . . . E-5
DALHART . . . C-1
DALLAS . . . F-3
DECATUR . . . E-3
DEL RIO . . . D-5
DENISON . . . F-2
DENTON . . . F-3
DICKENS . . . D-3
DILLEY . . . E-6
DIMMITT . . . C-2
DRYDEN . . . C-5
DUMAS . . . C-1
EAGLE PASS . . . D-6
EDEN . . . D-4
EDINBURG . . . E-7
EDNA . . . F-5
EL PASO . . . A-3
ELDORADO . . . D-4
ENCINAL . . . D-6
ENCINO . . . E-7
FABENS . . . A-4
FALFURRIAS . . . E-6
FARWELL . . . C-2
FLOYDADA . . . C-2
FORT STOCKTON . . . B-4
FORT WORTH . . . E-3
FREDERICKSBURG . . . D-5
FREEPORT . . . G-5
FREER . . . E-6
FRIONA . . . C-2
GAINESVILLE . . . E-3
GALVESTON . . . G-5
GATESVILLE . . . E-4
GEORGE WEST . . . E-6
GIDDINGS . . . F-5
GOLDTHWAITE . . . E-4
GOLIAD . . . F-5
GREENVILLE . . . F-3
GUTHRIE . . . D-3
HARLINGEN . . . E-7
HASKELL . . . D-3
HEARNE . . . F-4
HEMPSTEAD . . . F-5
HENDERSON . . . G-3
HENRIETTA . . . E-2
HEREFORD . . . C-2
HEWITT . . . E-4
HICO . . . E-4
HILLSBORO . . . E-4
HONDO . . . D-5
HOUSTON . . . F-5
HUNTSVILLE . . . F-4
JACKSBORO . . . E-3
JACKSONVILLE . . . G-3
JASPER . . . G-4
JEFFERSON . . . G-3
JOHNSON CITY . . . E-5
JUNCTION . . . D-4
KATY . . . F-5
KENEDY . . . E-6
KERMIT . . . B-4
KERRVILLE . . . D-5
KILGORE . . . G-3
KILLEEN . . . E-4
KINGSVILLE . . . E-6
LA GRANGE . . . F-5
LAMESA . . . C-3
LAMPASAS . . . E-4
LAREDO . . . D-6
LEAKEY . . . D-5
LEVELLAND . . . C-3
LITTLEFIELD . . . C-2
LIVINGSTON . . . G-4
LONGVIEW . . . G-3
LUBBOCK . . . C-3
LUFKIN . . . G-4
LULING . . . E-5
MADISONVILLE . . . F-4
MARATHON . . . B-5
MARFA . . . B-5
MARLIN . . . F-4
MASON . . . D-4
MATADOR . . . D-2
MCALLEN . . . E-7
MCCAMEY . . . C-4
MEMPHIS . . . D-2
MENARD . . . D-4
MERTZON . . . C-4
MEXIA . . . F-4
MIAMI . . . D-1
MIDLAND . . . C-3
MINEOLA . . . F-3
MISSION . . . E-7
MISSOURI CITY . . . F-5
MONAHANS . . . B-4
MOUNT PLEASANT . . . G-3
MULESHOE . . . C-2
NACOGDOCHES . . . G-4
NAVASOTA . . . F-4
NEW BRAUNFELS . . . E-5
NIXON . . . E-5
ODESSA . . . C-4
OLTON . . . C-2
ORANGE . . . G-5
PADUCAH . . . D-2
PALACIOS . . . F-6
PALESTINE . . . F-4
PAMPA . . . C-1
PARIS . . . F-2
PASADENA . . . G-5
PEARSALL . . . E-5
PECOS . . . B-4
PERRYTON . . . D-1
PLAINVIEW . . . C-2
PLEASANTON . . . E-5
PORT ARTHUR . . . G-5
PORT ISABEL . . . F-7
PORT LAVACA . . . F-6
PORTLAND . . . F-6
POST . . . C-3
PRESIDIO . . . B-5
RALLS . . . C-3
RANKIN . . . C-4
RAYMONDVILLE . . . E-7
REFUGIO . . . F-6
RICHMOND . . . F-5
RIO GRANDE CITY . . . E-7
ROBSTOWN . . . E-6
ROCKDALE . . . F-4
ROCKPORT . . . F-6
ROUND ROCK . . . E-4
RUSK . . . G-4
SAN ANGELO . . . D-4
SAN ANTONIO . . . E-5
SAN AUGUSTINE . . . G-4
SAN BENITO . . . E-7
SAN MARCOS . . . E-5
SANDERSON . . . C-5
SARITA . . . E-7
SEALY . . . F-5
SEGUIN . . . E-5
SEMINOLE . . . C-3
SEYMOUR . . . D-3
SHERMAN . . . F-2
SIERRA BLANCA . . . A-4
SILSBEE . . . G-4
SINTON . . . E-6
SLATON . . . C-3
SNYDER . . . D-3
SOCORRO . . . A-4
SONORA . . . D-4
STAMFORD . . . D-3
STANTON . . . C-3
STEPHENVILLE . . . E-3
STERLING CITY . . . C-4
STRATFORD . . . C-1
STUDY BUTTE . . . B-5
SULPHUR SPRINGS . . . F-3
SWEETWATER . . . D-3
TAYLOR . . . E-4
TEMPLE . . . E-4
TERRELL . . . F-3
TEXARKANA . . . G-2
THROCKMORTON . . . E-3
TULIA . . . C-2
TYLER . . . F-3
UVALDE . . . D-5
VAN HORN . . . B-4
VERNON . . . D-2
VICTORIA . . . F-6
WACO . . . F-4
WAXAHACHIE . . . F-3
WHARTON . . . F-5
WHEELER . . . D-1
WICHITA FALLS . . . E-2
WOODVILLE . . . G-4
ZAPATA . . . D-7
ZAVALLA . . . G-4

INDEX

UTAH

BIG WATER B-7
BLANDING E-6
BLUFF D-6
BOUNTIFUL B-2
CASTLE DALE C-4
COALVILLE C-2
COLTON C-4
COVE FORT B-5
CRESCENT JUNCTION D-5
DELTA B-4
DUCHESNE D-3
DUTCH JOHN E-2
EMERY C-5
EPHRAIM C-4
EUREKA B-3
FAIRVIEW C-4
FERRON C-5
FILLMORE B-5
FREMONT JUNCTION C-5
FRUITLAND D-4
GARDEN CITY C-1
GLENDALE B-6
GREEN RIVER D-4
GUNNISON C-4
HATCH B-6
HEBER CITY C-3
HELPER C-4
HOLDEN B-4
HUNTINGTON C-5
HURRICANE A-7
JUNCTION B-5
KANAB B-7
LAYTON B-2
LOGAN C-2
LYNNDYL B-4
MEXICAN HAT D-7
MOAB E-5
MONTICELLO D-6
MORGAN C-2
MOUNT CARMEL B-7
MYTON D-3
NEPHI B-4
OGDEN B-2
PANGUITCH B-6
PINTURA A-6
PRICE C-4
PROVO C-3
RICHMOND B-1
ROOSEVELT D-3
ROY B-2
SALINA C-5
SALT LAKE CITY C-3
SANDY C-3
SCIPIO B-4
SNOWVILLE B-1
SPANISH FORK B-3
SPRINGVILLE C-3
ST. GEORGE A-7
TREMONTON B-2
VERNAL E-3
WELLINGTON D-4
WENDOVER A-3

VERMONT

ALBURG A-1
BARRE A-3
BENNINGTON A-7
BRANDON A-4
BRATTLEBORO B-7
BURLINGTON A-2
CHARLOTTE A-3
CHESTER B-6
ESSEX JUNCTION A-2
GRAND ISLE A-2
LANCASTER D-2
LUDLOW B-5
MARSHFIELD B-3
MIDDLEBURY A-3
MONTPELIER B-3
NORTH STRATFORD D-1
NORTON D-1
RUTLAND B-5
SHELBURNE A-3
ST. JOHNSBURY D-2
VERGENNES A-3
WALLINGFORD A-5
WILMINGTON B-7
WOODSTOCK B-5

VIRGINIA

ABINGDON B-4
ACCOMAC G-3
ALEXANDRIA F-1
ALTAVISTA D-3
AMHERST D-3
ARLINGTON F-1
ASHLAND E-2
BEDFORD D-3
BIG STONE GAP A-3
BLACKSBURG C-3
BLUEFIELD C-3
BOWLING GREEN F-2
BOYCE E-1
BRISTOL B-4
BROOKNEAL E-3
BUENA VISTA D-3
CHARLOTTESVILLE E-2
CHATHAM D-4
CHESAPEAKE G-4
CLARKSVILLE E-4
COVINGTON C-3
CREWE E-3
CUCKOO E-2
CULPEPER E-1
CUMBERLAND E-3
DANVILLE D-4
EASTVILLE G-3
EMPORIA F-3
EXMORE G-3
FORK UNION E-3
FRANKLIN F-4
FRANKLIN D-2
FREDERICKSBURG E-2
GATE CITY B-4
HAMPTON G-3
HANOVER F-3
HANSONVILLE B-3
HARRISONBURG E-2
HILLSVILLE C-4
HOPEWELL F-3
INDEPENDENCE C-4
KIPTOPEKE G-3
LEESBURG E-1
LEXINGTON D-3
LOVINGTON E-3
LYNCHBURG D-3
MARTINSVILLE D-4
MIDDLEBURG E-1
MONTEREY D-2
NEW MARKET E-1
NEWPORT NEWS F-3
NORFOLK F-3
PETERSBURG F-3
PORTSMOUTH F-3
RADFORD C-3
REEDVILLE F-2
RICHMOND F-3
ROANOKE D-3
ROCKY MOUNT D-3
RUSTBURG D-3
SALUDA F-3
SOUTH BOSTON E-4
SOUTH HILL E-4
SPERRYVILLE E-2
STANARDSVILLE E-2
STAUNTON D-2
STUART C-4
SUFFOLK F-4
TAPPAHANNOCK F-2
TAZEWELL B-3
TROUTVILLE D-3
VANSANT B-3
VIRGINIA BEACH G-3
WARM SPRINGS D-2
WARRENTON E-1
WAVERLY F-3
WAYNESBORO D-2
WINCHESTER E-1
WISE B-3
WYLLIESBURG E-4
WYTHEVILLE B-3

WASHINGTON

ABERDEEN A-3
ALMIRA E-2
ANACORTES B-1
AUBURN B-2
BELLEVUE C-2
BELLINGHAM B-1
BLAINE B-1
BREMERTON B-2
BREWSTER E-2
CATHLAMET B-4
CENTRALIA B-3
CHEHALIS B-3
CHELAN E-2
CHEWELAH F-2
CLARKSTON G-4
CLE ELUM D-3
COLFAX G-3
COLVILLE F-1
CONNELL E-3
COUNTRY HOMES G-2
DAVENPORT F-2
DAYTON F-4
EDMONDS B-2
ELLENSBURG D-3
ELMA B-3
ENTIAT D-2
EPHRATA E-3
EVERETT C-2
FEDERAL WAY B-3
FERNDALE B-1
FORKS A-2
FRIDAY HARBOR B-1
GEORGE E-3
GOLD BAR C-2
GOLDENDALE D-4
GRANDVIEW D-4
HOODSPORT B-3
HOQUIAM A-3
KALAMA B-4
KELSO B-4
KENNEWICK E-4
LACEY B-3
LAGRANDE B-3
LEAVENWORTH D-2
LONGVIEW B-4
MARYSVILLE C-2
MESA E-3
MINERAL C-3
MORTON C-4
MOSES LAKE E-3
MOUNT VERNON B-1
MUKILTEO C-2
NEAH BAY A-1
NEWPORT G-2
OAK HARBOR B-2
OCEAN PARK A-4
OCEAN SHORES A-3
OKANOGAN E-2
OLYMPIA B-3
OMAK E-1
OPPORTUNITY G-2
OROVILLE E-1
OTHELLO E-3
PACKWOOD C-4
PASCO E-4
POMEROY G-4
PORT ANGELES B-2
PORT HADLOCK B-2
PORT TOWNSEND B-2
PROSSER E-4
PULLMAN G-3
QUINCY E-3
RAYMOND A-3
REDMOND C-2
RENTON C-2
RICHLAND E-4
RIMROCK D-3
RITZVILLE F-3
ROSALIA F-3
SEATTLE B-2
SEQUIM B-2
SHELTON B-3
SKYKOMISH C-2
SNOHOMISH C-2
SOUTH CLE ELUM D-3
SPANAWAY C-3
SPOKANE F-2
SPRAGUE F-3
SUMNER C-3
SUNNYSIDE E-4
SYDNEY B-1
TACOMA B-3
TAHOLAH A-3
TOLEDO B-4
TOPPENISH D-4
TUMWATER B-3
VANCOUVER B-5
WALLA WALLA F-4
WAPATO D-4
WENATCHEE D-3
WHITE SALMON C-5
WILBUR F-2
YAKIMA D-4

WEST VIRGINIA

ANSTED B-4
BRIDGEPORT D-3
BUCKHANNON C-3
CAMERON C-2
CHARLESTON B-4
CLARKSBURG C-3
DELBARTON A-5
ELKINS D-3
FAIRMONT C-3
FRANKLIN D-4
GILBERT B-5
GRAFTON D-3
HARMAN D-3
HARPERS FERRY F-3
HARTS A-5
HILLSBORO D-5
HUNTINGTON A-4
HUTTONSVILLE C-4
KERMIT A-5
KEYSER E-3
LEON B-4
LEWISBURG C-5
MARTINSBURG F-3
MOOREFIELD E-3
MORGANTOWN D-2
MOUNDSVILLE C-2
MOUNT NEBO C-5
NEW MARTINSVILLE C-2
OAK HILL B-5
PARKERSBURG B-3
PHILIPPI D-3
POINT PLEASANT A-4
PRINCETON B-6
RAINELLE C-5
RAVENSWOOD B-3
ROMNEY E-3
SOPHIA B-5
SPENCER B-4
UNION C-5
WELCH B-6
WHEELING C-2

WISCONSIN

ANTIGO C-3
APPLETON D-4
ASHLAND B-1
BARABOO C-5
BEAVER DAM C-5
BELOIT C-6
BLACK RIVER FALLS B-3
BRUCE B-3
BRULE B-1
CAMERON B-3
CHILTON D-4
CHIPPEWA FALLS B-3
CLINTONVILLE D-3
COLOMA C-4
COLUMBUS C-5
CRANDON D-3
CRIVITZ D-3
DENMARK D-4
DICKEYVILLE B-6
DODGEVILLE B-5
EAGLE RIVER C-2
EAU CLAIRE A-3
ELKHORN D-5
ELLSWORTH A-3
FOND DU LAC D-4
FORT ATKINSON D-5
FRIENDSHIP C-4
GALESVILLE B-4
GRAFTON D-5
GREEN BAY D-3
HAYWARD B-2
KENOSHA D-6
LA CROSSE B-4
LADYSMITH B-3
LAND O' LAKES C-2
LAONA D-2
MADISON C-5
MANITOWOC D-4
MARINETTE D-3
MARION C-3
MARSHFIELD B-3
MAUSTON B-4
MEDFORD B-3
MELLEN B-2
MENASHA C-4
MERRILL C-3
MILWAUKEE D-5
MONROE C-5
NEILLSVILLE B-4
NEW LONDON C-4
OCONTO D-3
OSHKOSH C-4
PEMBINE D-2
PITTSVILLE C-4
PLATTEVILLE B-5
PLOVER C-4
PORT WASHINGTON D-5
PORTAGE C-5
PRAIRIE DU CHIEN B-5
PRENTICE C-2
RACINE D-5
READSTOWN B-5
RICE LAKE B-3
RICHLAND CENTER B-5
SAUK CITY C-5
SCHOFIELD C-3
SHAWANO D-3
SHEBOYGAN D-4
SPARTA B-4
SPOONER A-2
STEVENS POINT C-4
SUPERIOR A-1
TURTLE LAKE A-3
UNITY C-3
VIROQUA B-5
WAUKESHA D-5
WAUPACA C-4
WAUPUN C-4
WAUSAU C-3
WAUSAUKEE D-3
WEST BEND D-5
WISCONSIN DELLS C-4
WITTENBERG C-3

WYOMING

AFTON A-3
ALCOVA E-3
ALPINE A-3
ARLINGTON E-4
BAGGS D-5
BANNER D-1
BONDURANT B-3
BORDER A-4
BOSLER F-4
BUFFALO E-2
BURRIS C-2
CASPER E-3
CHEYENNE F-5
CHUGWATER F-4
CODY B-1
COKEVILLE A-3
CRESTON JUNCTION D-4
CROWHEART B-2
DANIEL B-3
DEAVER C-1
DOUGLAS F-3
DUBOIS B-2
EDEN C-4
ELK MOUNTAIN E-4
EMBLEM C-1
EVANSTON A-5
FARSON B-4
FORT WASHAKIE C-3
FOUR CORNERS F-2
FREEDOM A-3
GILLETTE E-1
GLENDO F-3
GREEN RIVER B-4
GREYBULL D-1
GROVER A-3
HANNA E-4
JACKSON B-2
JAY EM G-3
KAYCEE E-2
KEMMERER B-4
KIRBY D-2
LAMONT D-4
LANDER C-3
LARAMIE F-4
LITTLE AMERICA B-4
LOVELL D-1
LUSK F-3
LYMAN B-5
MAMMOTH A-1
MANDERSON D-1
MERIDEN F-4
MONETA D-3
MOORCROFT F-1
MORAN B-2
MUDDY GAP D-3
NATRONA E-3
NEWCASTLE F-2
OPAL B-4
ORIN F-3
PINE BLUFFS G-5
PINEDALE B-3
POINT OF ROCKS C-4
RANCHESTER D-1
RAWLINS C-4
REDBIRD F-2
RIVERTON C-3
RIVERVIEW F-2
ROCK RIVER E-4
ROCK SPRINGS C-4
SAGE A-4
SHERIDAN D-1
SHOSHONI D-2
SLATER F-4
SUNDANCE F-1
SWEETWATER STATION D-3
TEN SLEEP D-2
THAYNE A-3
THERMOPOLIS D-2
TORRINGTON F-4
TOWER JUNCTION B-1
UPTON F-2
VAN TASSELL G-3
WALCOTT C-4
WALTMAN D-3
WHEATLAND F-4
WINCHESTER C-2
WORLAND D-2

CANADA

ALMA E-4
ARCTIC BAY D-1
ARVIAT D-2
BAKER LAKE C-1
BATHURST INLET C-1
BRANDON B-4
CALGARY B-3
CAMBRIDGE BAY C-1
CAMPBELL RIVER A-3
CAPE DORSET D-1
CAPE DYER E-1
CARMACKS A-2
CHANNEL-PORT-AUX-BASQUES G-4
CHARLOTTETOWN F-4
CHESTERFIELD INLET C-2
CHIBOUGAMAU E-4
CHISASIBI E-3
CHURCHILL D-3
CLYDE RIVER E-1
COPPERMINE C-1
CORAL HARBOUR D-2
CORNER BROOK G-4
DAWSON A-1
DAWSON CREEK B-3
DEASE LAKE A-2
EDMONTON B-3
FARO B-1
FLIN FLON C-3
FORT FRANKLIN B-1
FORT GOOD HOPE B-1
FORT MCMURRAY B-3
FORT MCPHERSON B-1
FORT SEVERN D-3
FORT SIMPSON B-2
FORT SMITH C-2
FREDERICTON F-4
GASPE F-4
GRAND FALLS G-3
GRANDE PRAIRIE B-3
HALIFAX F-4
HAPPY VALLEY-GOOSE BAY F-3
HAY RIVER B-2
HOLMAN B-1
HOPEDALE F-3
IGLOOLIK D-1
INUKJUAK E-3
INUVIK B-1
IQALUIT E-2
IVUJIVIK E-2
KAMLOOPS A-3
KAPUSKASING E-4
KENORA D-4
KITIMAT A-2
KUUJJUAQ F-3
LA RONGE C-3
LABRADOR CITY E-3
LAKE HARBOUR E-2
LETHBRIDGE B-4
LONDON E-5
MARYSTOWN G-4
MEANDER RIVER B-2
MONCTON F-4
MONTRÉAL E-4
MOOSONEE D-4
NAIN F-2
NORTH BAY E-4
OTTAWA E-4
PANGNIRTUNG E-1
PEACE RIVER B-3
PELLY BAY D-1
PICKLE LAKE D-4
PORT BUNWELL F-2
PORT HARDY A-3
PORT INLET D-1
PRINCE ALBERT C-3
PRINCE GEORGE A-3
PRINCE RUPERT A-2
QUAQTAQ E-2
QUÉBEC E-4
QUEEN CHARLOTTE A-2
RED DEER B-3
RED LAKE D-4
REGINA C-4
REPULSE BAY D-2
RESOLUTION ISLAND F-2
RIVIÈRE-DU-LOUP F-4
ROUYN-NORANDA E-4
SAINT JOHN F-4
SASKATOON C-3
SAULT STE. MARIE D-4
SHERBROOKE E-4
SPENCE BAY D-1
ST. ANTHONY G-3
ST. JOHN'S G-4
SWIFT CURRENT B-4
SYDNEY G-4
TESLIN A-2
THE PAS C-3
THOMPSON C-3
THUNDER BAY D-4
TIMMINS D-4
TORONTO E-5
TRAIL B-3
TROIS-RIVIERES E-4
TRURO G-4
TUNGSTEN B-1
TWIN FALLS F-3
URANIUM CITY C-2
VANCOUVER A-3
VICTORIA A-3
WATSON LAKE A-2
WAWA D-4
WHITEHORSE A-1
WILLIAMS LAKE A-3
WINDSOR E-5
WINNIPEG C-4
YARMOUTH F-4
YELLOWKNIFE C-2
YORK FACTORY D-3

MEXICO

ACAPONETA C-3
ACAPULCO D-5
AGUACALIENTES C-3
ALVARADO F-4
CAMPECHE G-4
CANCUN G-3
CARAPAN D-4
CHETUMAL G-4
CHIHUAHUA C-2
CIUDAD CAMARGO C-2
CIUDAD CONSTITUCIÓN A-3
CIUDAD MADERO E-3
CIUDAD MANTE D-3
CIUDAD OBREGON B-2
CIUDAD VICTORIA D-3
COLIMA D-4
CUERNAVACA D-4
CULIACÁN C-3
DURANGO C-3
ENSENADA A-1
ESCÁRCEGA G-4
FELIPE CARRILLO PUERTO G-4
FRESNILLO C-3
GUADALAJARA C-4
GUAYMAS B-2
HERMOSILO B-2
JIMÉNEZ C-2
JUÁREZ C-1
JUCHITAN F-5
LA PAZ B-3
LEON D-4
LOS MOCHIS C-2
MANZANILLO C-4
MATAMOROS E-2
MAZATLÁN C-3
MÉRIDA F-3
MEXICALI A-1
MEXICO CITY D-4
MONTERREY D-3
MORELIA D-4
NAVOJOA B-2
NOGALES B-1
NUEVO LAREDO D-2
OAXACA E-4
PACHUCA D-4
PETO G-4
PLAYA AZUL D-4
PUEBLA E-4
SAN CRISTÓBAL DE LAS CASAS F-4
SAN LUIS POTOSÍ D-3
SANTA ROSALÍA A-2
SATILLO E-3
TAMPICO E-3
TAPACHULA F-5
TEHUACÁN E-4
TEHUANTEPEC E-5
TEPIC C-4
TIJUANA A-1
TORREON C-3
TUXPAN E-3
TUXTEPEC F-4
TUXTLA GUTIERREZ F-4
VALLADOLID G-3
VERACRUZ F-4
ZACATECAS C-3

ANSWER PAGE

Page 3

SELMA / MONTGOMERY / PHENIX CITY / TUSCALOOSA / DOTHAN

Page 4

Page 6
Hot Springs

Page 8
1. Wyoming
2. Nebraska
3. Kansas
4. New Mexico
5. Arizona
6. Utah
7. Oklahoma

Page 10
14

Page 11

Page 12

PEACH

Page 13

_____
_____
_____
_____
_____
_____
_____
_____
_____
_____
_____
_____

Page 14

Page 15

Champaign	D-4
Chicago	D-1
Decatur	C-4
Paris	D-4
Rock Falls	C-2
Springfield	B-4
Waterloo	B-6

Page 17

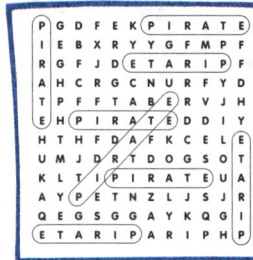

Page 18
Wyatt Earp

Page 19
Daniel Boone

Page 20

Page 21

Page 22

Page 24
THE GREAT LAKES

MICHIGAN / ONTARIO / HURON / SUPERIOR / ERIE

Page 25
St. Cloud
Red Wing
Jackson
Cook
Duluth

Page 26

Page 27
1. East
2. 40
3. Star
4. Illinois

Page 28
Cowboy

Page 29

63

ANSWER PAGE

Page 30

Austin	C-3
Carson City	A-4
Eureka	C-3
Jackpot	D-1
Reno	A-3
Sparks	A-3
Topaz Lake	A-4

Page 34

```
        C A M D E N
        T
C H E S T E R R E N T O N
        A           E
        N C C I T Y W
        T           B
O C E A N C I T Y   R
        C           U
        Y           N
                    S
                    W
                    I
                    C
                    K
```

Page 35

Page 37
Kitty Hawk

Page 39
fall football

Page 40

_____

_____

_____

_____

_____

_____

_____

_____

Page 41

Page 42
Punxsutawney Phil

Page 44

Page 45
Mount Rushmore

Page 46
Drums

Page 47

Page 48

Page 50
1. Roanoke
2. North Carolina
3. True
4. 33
5. West Virginia
6. Atlantic

Page 51
1. Yakima
2. Seattle
3. Spokane
4. Everett
5. Olympia
6. Tacoma

Page 52

Page 53

Page 54
1. Cheyenne
2. Rawlins
3. Jackson
4. Laramie
5. Sundance

Page 55

Page 40
Bale of hay
Indian
Pickup
Truck
Headdress
Rooster
Oil Well
Pig
Bird
Pitchfork

Page 13
Sea Shell
Palm Tree
Beach Ball
Starfish
Flower
Sparky
Volcano
Suntan
Lotion
Whale
Sea Turtle
Fish
Sunglasses